Going for the
Green

Going for the Green

Green

Prepare Your Body, Mind, and Swing for Winning Golf

Gary Gilchrist   Susan Hill   Jeff Troesch

Foreword by Suzann Pettersen,
Winner of the Michelob Ultra and McDonald's LPGA Championship

STERLING

New York / London
www.sterlingpublishing.com

STERLING and the distinctive Sterling logo are registered trademarks of
Sterling Publishing Co., Inc.

Library of Congress Cataloging-in-Publication Data

Gilchrist, Gary.
  Going for the green : prepare your body, mind, and swing for winning
golf / Gary Gilchrist, Susan Hill, and Jeff Troesch ; foreword by
Suzann Pettersen.
        p. cm.
    Includes index.
    ISBN 978-1-4027-4769-4
  1. Golf--Training. 2. Swing (Golf) 3. Golf--Psychological aspects.
I. Hill, Susan, 1962- II. Troesch, Jeff. III. Title.
  GV979.T68G53 2009
  796.352--dc22

                                        2008035256

10 9 8 7 6 5 4 3 2 1

Published by Sterling Publishing Co., Inc.
387 Park Avenue South, New York, NY 10016
Copyright © 2009 Gary Gilchrist, Susan Hill, and Jeff Troesch
Distributed in Canada by Sterling Publishing
c/o Canadian Manda Group, 165 Dufferin Street
Toronto, Ontario, Canada M6K 3H6
Distributed in the United Kingdom by GMC Distribution Services
Castle Place, 166 High Street, Lewes, East Sussex, England BN7 1XU
Distributed in Australia by Capricorn Link (Australia) Pty. Ltd.
P.O. Box 704, Windsor, NSW 2756, Australia

Book design and layout: Gavin Motnyk

Photography credits: Studio 404 Photography Alan Huestis

Sterling ISBN 978-1-4027-4769-4

For information about custom editions, special sales, premium and
corporate purchases, please contact Sterling Special Sales
Department at 800-805-5489 or specialsales@sterlingpublishing.com.

Contents

Foreword by Suzann Pettersen   *vii*

Introduction by Gary Gilchrist   1

Chapter One: Periodization Training   5

Chapter Two: Elements of a Complete Golfer   17

Chapter Three: Assess Your Game   25

Chapter Four: Technical Phase   53

Chapter Five: Pre-competition Phase   101

Chapter Six: Competition Phase   141

Chapter Seven: Active Rest and Regeneration Phase   163

Appendix   *169*

Golf Resources   *182*

Index   *185*

About the Authors   *195*

Picture Credits   *199*

Foreword

I majored in social studies and history in undergraduate school and at the master's level. I have always loved sports and competing. Until I was 12 years old I played many different sports, including skiing, ice skating, horse riding, gymnastics, and soccer. My love for sport gave me a great athletic foundation and has helped me tremendously in my golf career.

I thrive on challenge and strive for excellence. My goal is to always be 100 percent prepared in body and mind for peak performance. To me this means being the best-trained athlete on tour, having a game that works under pressure, and being mentally in a place that has no limitations. I work on this process daily to prepare myself for every fitness session, every shot I make, and every decision to which I commit. Golf is more than a game; it is a never-ending process of becoming better and reaching new heights. That is what drives me—becoming the best player in the world.

What is really important to me is having a strong belief in every aspect of my game and a strong support system that gives me energy. In early 2007 I put together a new team with Gary as my swing coach. When we first worked together, I was amazed at Gary's approach to teaching. His philosophy focuses on feel, preparation, and following a periodized approach to training as much as it does on technique, which is so important in competition. He made some basic adjustments to my swing and gave me a fresh perspective on my game. Those insights and changes in my preparation have allowed me to enjoy my most successful year on tour, which included my first "major" win at the McDonald's LPGA Championship.

Going for the Green is a book for all levels of golfers. You may not want to be the best golfer in the world, but I'm sure you want to improve. The information in this book will give you the tools you need to be a better golfer and a better athlete. Apply these techniques and you will achieve results that you didn't think were possible!

Suzann Pettersen
Winner of the 2007 Michelob ULTRA Open,
McDonald's LPGA Championship, Longs Drug
Challenge, and Hana Bank-KOLON Championship

Introduction

by Gary Gilchrist

Walk down the driving range at any professional golf event, and it's clear that the world's best players don't become stars all by themselves. The more famous the player, the more likely he or she is accompanied by prominent support personnel—a swing coach, personal fitness trainer, and mental consultant, to name a few. From the other side of the ropes, an average golfer gazes at that scene and thinks, "I wonder how good I'd be if I had access to that kind of advice."

Whether you are one of many casual golf fans who are simply curious about why the best players in the world rose to the top while others have not, or a serious competitor of the game, this book was written to provide a unique insider's look at the world of top-level golf training.

My experience in teaching some of the world's best golfers began with my position as the Director of Instruction for the David Leadbetter Junior Golf Academy in Bradenton, Florida. I was trained as a technical teacher but quickly realized that to develop golfers to the next level, they needed to master more than just technique—they needed a comprehensive training program that incorporated every aspect of being a champion. I also realized that I needed to be a "coach" and not just an instruc-

tor, and this was very unique to golf instruction at the time. Learning from other sports like tennis, I developed a golf training system that combined the three most important areas of the game: technical skill, physical fitness, and mental conditioning.

The academy quickly became the leader in junior golf training, and I fulfilled my dream of taking young players from one level to the next and seeing them mature to the top of their field. I have worked and supported the careers of many of today's top golfers, including Paula Creamer, Michelle Wie, Julieta Granada, Peter Hedblom, Sean O'Hair, Nicole Perrot, Suzann Pettersen, and Candy Hannemann. These players have all used this system to maintain a high level of performance in golf.

The purpose of the training program is to accelerate development and prepare the golfer to peak at the right time. Winning comes from taking the golfer through high- and low-intensity training while challenging them to mentally focus and concentrate on completing the task at hand. I am a strong believer in giving my students a program versus a lesson. Going for the Green means to think, practice, and prepare with a purpose. This will give you the confidence you need to reach your full potential and achieve your goals. The success of this program speaks

for itself and will help golfers of all levels. I have watched this system positively impact recreational, junior, amateur, college, and professional golfers by giving them the tools they need to perform at the highest levels.

Going for the Green takes average golfers through the various training phases step by step, starting with the basics and working up to more advanced drills and exercises. For the first time, the average golfer will be offered complete access to information the pros use to raise and maintain their performance.

We have broken down some of the most complex training regimens into an easy-to-follow program. The key concept in the book is "periodization," which refers to a rotating cycle of optimal training plans that coincides with a player's performance goals. Tiger Woods was one of the first golfers to use periodization to map out his season schedule with the goal of reaching his peak performance during major championships.

Periodization is now being taught to competitive players at all levels and is especially popular

in the collegiate and junior ranks. While many of these players hope to earn fame and fortune on the professional tours, recreational golfers with more modest improvement standards can use the same training approach to reach their goals. My experience says it is just as effective for those with a high handicap as it is for those with a low handicap. Of course, the real improvement any golfer experiences will be reflected in each player's personal performance goals, level of discipline, and commitment to the improvement process.

Success in golf can be fleeting, but the training program in Going for the Green has a solid foundation that ensures its longevity. The techniques are adaptable to just about any golfer, even without access to all the training aids and video equipment used by the experts. In Going for the Green, the swing coach, fitness trainer, and psychology expert all come to you rather than you having to go to them, providing you with the ultimate training program to help you reach a new level of performance.

Train like a champion!

Chapter 1

Periodization Training

Golfers are dreamers. They dream of hitting every drive in the middle of the fairway, flying every iron shot toward the flag, and rolling every putt into the hole. Dreaming is a prerequisite for those who play a game in which complete mastery is unattainable, even for famous pros such as Tiger Woods and Annika Sörenstam. The pursuit of that elusive goal provides a thrill for millions of avid golfers who feel an unmistakable joy after launching a perfectly struck shot or sinking a long putt. They know at that moment that they did everything right. Now the challenge is to step up to the next shot and try to do it again.

Today's golfers are savvier than ever. They have access to the world's best instructors and golf experts through numerous daily television broadcasts, various golf magazines, and the seemingly endless supply of free tips that can be viewed on the Internet. Now their dreams have expanded from notions of playing as "one-shot wonders" to being true artists of the game.

With this knowledge and with new role models on the tour, golfers now dream of winning local tournaments, whether they are charity golf tournaments, club championships, or corporate-sponsored events. Some golfers have even loftier goals, including winning a major junior golf event on the American Junior Golf Association or the International Junior Golf Tour and getting the attention of key college recruiters. Yet there are still others—hundreds of thousands of everyday golfers—who just want to learn how to play their very best golf on any given day. They simply want to maximize their talents in the time they are able to dedicate to their game.

For those golfers, there are questions that remain unanswered: How do golfers create peak performance for a specific tournament or work toward achieving their very best performance at specified dates throughout the competitive season? Can a collegiate golfer win in a crucial moment that helps his or her team or individual standing? What about the woman or man of any age at every local country club across the country who has dreamed of one day winning his or her club championship? Can they train in a certain way or prepare their bodies and minds in a way that will fulfill their dream on the day they choose?

When most golfers think of the elements of the game in which they want to improve, the vast majority think in terms of either technical elements or outcome: "I want to make more putts." "I want to hit more fairways." "I want to break 90 consistently."

Although they should not disregard these important considerations, players truly interested in overall improvement of their games would do well to consider paying attention to all aspects of the game of golf. Rather than dividing golf into full swing, short game, and putting, the more astute players recognize a division that has mechanical, physical, mental, and tactical components.

Many seek what they believe is the Holy Grail of a great golf swing (mechanical) or putting stroke (mechanical). This is done while ignoring the benefits of golf-specific fitness training, mental training, and/or course management improvement. The practice ranges around the world are full of players who hit ball after ball in an attempt to perfect their swing, only to find that when actually taken to the course, the improved swing alone is not enough to produce the results they desire.

It is a challenge for the serious player—let alone the casual player—to make the non-swing-related elements a priority. With a finite amount of time to devote to golf, most prefer to swing a club or stroke a putter rather than work on the fitness/mental/tactical fundamentals.

That being acknowledged, players would do well to ask themselves these questions and answer them honestly: "How much better would my score be if I were more physically flexible, were stronger, or had more stamina?" "If I were less distracted on the course—less nervous about short putts, more confident in my game—how would that affect my play?" "Am I sure that I am taking all considerations into account before I hit shots on the course?" "Would I be helped if I made better decisions while playing?"

Periodization

Periodization is fairly new to golf instruction, but it has been around much longer in sports such as marathon running, long-distance biking, and tennis. Think of Lance Armstrong preparing for the Tour de France or Pete Sampras being at his strongest for Grand Slam events. For a golfer in training, it is the critical element in reaching performance goals.

Improvement doesn't come from practicing all facets of the game at the same time. That would be counterproductive, not to mention confusing and impossible to schedule. This is where periodization comes in.

Periodization is a systematic approach to improving your game by dividing your training program into segments with the ultimate goal of creating peak performance at specific times of the year. The essence of periodization reflects a calculated, planned way to develop a golfer's game, taking into account where one's game is currently,

where one is attempting to go with one's game, and whether one is a high handicapper, scratch, or professional player trying to improve. Ultimately, it takes into account the mental, physical, and technical elements of the game.

From there, it is used to create a precise plan of action to make sure that the developmental process is as succinct, purposeful, thorough, and efficient as possible. The action plan involves looking at upcoming tournament opportunities, exploring various training options, and examining all the variables that ultimately affect a player's development.

A periodization plan often is devised for an entire year and implemented in several cycles and minicycles as one moves through each season. These cycles fluctuate in terms of intensity, volume of work, and type and style of training. They can be as short as days or weeks, often called "microcycles," or range from a number of months up to a year, commonly referred to as "macrocycles." Periodization programs also can be designed over several years for a golfer who has longer-term goals.

There is no question that most players want to play their very best every time they pick up their clubs. Realistically, though, everybody is different and each golfer has his or her own set of distractions, need for recovery, method for endurance building, and developmental process. All these components together make it virtually impossible for any person to dominate every time he or she plays. However, one can control the training elements that put him or her in a position of advantage during tournaments that really matter.

Most professional golfers focus their attention on achieving peak performance at the majors, where the rewards to golfers are the highest. Here is an example of how a microcycle may be used leading up to a major golf tournament such as the U.S. Open or the Masters. Typically for a major, if possible, players would find a time earlier in the year to play a practice round or two on the course in order to get the greatest sense of familiarity with the course possible. For example, as early as 2006, many PGA Tour players had taken trips to La Jolla, California, to play some rounds at Torrey Pines, site of the 2008 U.S. Open. Before the event, the players sometimes attempt to integrate certain equipment or shots into their repertoire in events that lead up to the major. As another example, leading up to the British Open, many players purposefully hit low knockdown and running shots in lead-up competitions despite the fact that the course on which they are playing may not dictate that kind of shot. This allows the player to put into competition the kinds of shots that are required on a windy course, as is typically found at the British Open. Also, there is typically no pro-am at major

events, and so the days during the week of the tournament are spent getting familiar with the course, with particular emphasis on getting more comfortable with hitting shots out of longer-than-typical rough and chipping and putting on faster-than-typical greens.

For a regular golf tournament, players typically arrive at the golf course on Monday and begin working with their instructors on specific drills, motions, and range time that are more technical in orientation. Tuesday is the day of their practice round, and so attention shifts to tournament preparation. On Wednesday, the player is either practicing or playing in a pro-am. By Thursday the players must be totally prepared to move into tournament competition. They literally follow a scheduled plan or an organized system that takes them through each phase of development, but all in one week. Each strategy session targets a different element of the game and a specific purpose for peak performance.

Here are some important guidelines typically used in scheduling and planning sessions within a microcycle:

- Be sure to schedule active recovery after physical, technical, or sensory overload days.
- Alternate high-intensity workouts with lower-intensity workouts.
- Avoid taxing the same energy system on consecutive days. This includes the same mental system as well as the same physical energy system.
- Balance the attention to the technical, physical, and mental components. It doesn't have to be an equal distribution, but it should be balanced in its approach.

Beginning with the End in Mind

Creating peak performance starts with an intimate knowledge of one's strengths and weaknesses. The key then becomes developing a clear plan for improvement. Great players understand the effort involved in advancing to the next level. To play consistently at your best, you have to develop a keen awareness of the things you do that allow you to play well. Reaching this goal of peak performance can take years of patience and persistence that will give you the skills to succeed. Many golfers simply seek more enjoyment of the game, and this also comes with seeing improvement and knowing that all the facets of your game are getting stronger.

All effective programs begin with a goal-setting period that is based on one's personal set criteria. Most players benefit from having specific goals to accomplish regarding the mental, physical, or technical facets of the game. Remember, a player's growth is dependent on his or her efforts.

This is the essence of periodization, and for a golfer in training it is the critical element in reaching performance goals. A properly prepared program to meet the needs, goals, and desires of a golfer at any level must begin with the end in mind. This is where the goal-setting process takes place and where golfers map out their specific dates of desired peak performance.

Phases of Competitive Golf
Assessment Phase

Whether one is referring to the technical, mental, or physical side of the game, the assessment period is among the most important. All golfers have specific genetic traits, skills, thought processes, and movement patterns that affect their approach to learning, understanding, and applying new principles to the way they perform a golf swing and play golf. Regardless of those individual characteristics, all golfers have areas of strengths and areas of weaknesses in regard to each of those elements.

The real secret is to perform a thorough assessment of the overall health of your game, your mind, and your body so that you can create a specific plan for improvement. Ultimately, every golfer must ask him- or herself, "What is really holding me back from playing my best golf?" The answer often lies in the assessment and understanding of one's individual strengths and weaknesses as a player.

Charles Staley, a widely recognized strength and conditioning coach, wrote, "Exploiting your opponent's weaknesses begins with identifying your own." There is an abundance of truth in this simple statement, especially as it pertains to golf. The idea of assessing one's weaknesses has long been the key to understanding how to perform at a higher level. In golf, it is not the most impactful way to achieve one's goals but the quickest and most efficient way.

Technical Phase

In golf, we can analyze every detail and component of our games from a technical, physical, and mental perspective. From our initial assessments, we can create a specific blueprint of player development that focuses on the areas in which we are weak. We then can set straightforward short-term and long-term goals with clear objectives.

The technical phase of training is critical because it is the foundation of training. This cycle is used to identify weakness in the technical areas of the swing and the short game and to make corrections in technique. The primary focus switches to body motion and efficient movement on both the technical and physical sides of the game. Often, players use training aids on the range and minimal weight in the gym to perform basic fundamental movement patterns. From a mental perspective, golfers are abandoning long-held belief systems and learning new thoughts and processes. During the initial technical phase, the basic fundamentals of the way the mind can affect the golfer are taught. Golfers then begin to understand how their outlook, preparation psychology, and physiology can affect their attitude, and their understanding of the process is defined clearly. The goal during this phase is to be extremely patient and disciplined throughout the process.

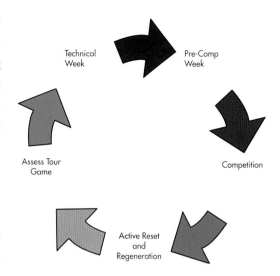

Technical Week

Pre-Comp Week

Competition

Active Reset and Regeneration

Assess Tour Game

Pre-competition Preparation

Many golfers see the assessment and technical phase of learning as the ultimate goal. Their goal is always technical because they get their confidence from ball striking. The key is to make sure they make the mental transition into the pre-competition phase. Whereas previous phases focused on learning new styles, traits, and patterns, this is the time to see their direct translation to the course. Golfers who have asked repeatedly, "Why can't I play like I practice?" will find all the answers here.

Golfers begin building on the new movement patterns learned in the previous phase of training. Technically speaking, golfers are exploring ways to shape new shots and prepare for competition. Their workouts become more challenging through increased volume, intensity, and workload.

Players also are developing mental and physical warm-up routines to improve their focus and ability to handle the pressure of intense competition. They learn relaxation and visualization techniques, becoming true strategists of the game.

Competition Phase

By this time, golfers have their game plan and are ready for peak performance. All technical work takes a backseat as golfers now carry with them confidence from their preparation and a mental belief in themselves. The majority of the hard work has been done in previous stages, and so the competition phase allows players to see the outcome of their efforts.

Players have developed their pre-shot routine, which will give them a laserlike focus and integrate the "one-shot-at-a-time model" to help them maneuver through competitive pressures. They continue to maintain their golf fitness programs, but the intensity is lowered and their entire focus is on the task at hand.

Active Rest and Regeneration

Rest, recovery, and regeneration of the mind, body, and spirit are now well deserved. Golfers can relax, put their clubs aside for a short while, and begin the process of reflection—what went right, what went wrong, how to improve going back into competition.

There will always be advocates of constantly continuing the training pressure—to not let up, push through adversity, and never rest—but the majority of golfers and other successful athletes have learned that rest and regeneration are just as important to performance as they are to any other phase of training.

For those who have difficulty "letting go" in this stage, remember that you can continue to play golf, exercise, and reach for your dreams while still keeping a relaxed attitude and state of mind.

The Purpose and the Process

Those very first steps in the periodized training model attempt to "shock" the system physically and mentally so that the body and mind can create new stimuli for learning and growing. As with all things, once the body gets accustomed to these changes, new stimuli are needed for further change and development. Thus, the body undergoes a new series of imposed stresses as a learning tool and then finds a way to adapt to those changes. New training variables always are introduced in stages and in numerous ways to keep the body responding and continuing to develop in strength and stamina.

Transitional Preparation

Preparation can take several different forms. Most common in a periodized golf program is the primary introduction of "general" preparation. General preparation for your game may include learning new techniques in your swing by concentrating on the motion and new changes as opposed to ball flight. In a physical sense, golfers should focus on proper form and movement patterns when learning new exercises, focus on training the dominant energy system, gaining muscle, or losing excess body fat. Learning basic body positions will serve as the foundation for all future movement. From a mental perspective, general preparation can include learning the one-shot-at-a-time model or the importance of breathing and its effect on one's physiology. Although each of these preparation styles will enhance one's level of play, they are general in their approach.

Contrast this with "specific" preparation. This transition signals the need for more golf-specific positions, drills, movements, and thought processes. As the season moves closer to competition, the body and mind are making the transition in a step-by-step building process. Volume and effort typically increase as a golfer moves from general preparation to specific preparation. Exercise helps the transition from increasing flexibility and mobility to a concentrated focus on developing more speed and power.

Evaluating Golf Performance

The goal of the whole periodization model is to be in a constant mode of evaluation, corrective action, and process orientation. This system has been proved over time and in both business and sports models. Not only does it produce the best results, it does so in the shortest period of time and with the least amount of frustration.

Statistics accumulated on the game of golf have shown that average male and female handicaps in this country haven't changed in over a decade. Fifteen years ago the average handicap for a male was 16.2 and the average for a female was 29. These figures still stand as the average handicaps for males and females. Yet we know more about the game of golf today and have made significant advances in golf equipment and ball technology. How can golfers reasonably expect to see a change in their game unless they look at their approach to learning from a different perspective?

As we delve into the mechanics of developing a golfer's game in a step-by-step process throughout this book, keep in mind the primary goal of periodization and the way we will move full circle toward peak performance. The following diagram sums up the circular process of development, beginning with making "performance observations."

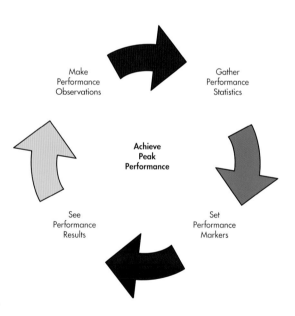

Example of a One-Day Microcycle

Cycles can be designed for any length of time and have been proven effective for times of as little as one day. Remember that the continuum is the same: assessment, technical, pre-comp, competition, and active rest.

Let's assume you've determined that putting is clearly a weak link for you. Here's an example of what a one-day minicycle might look like for you.

Sample Putting Practice

- 30 minutes: Spend a half hour focusing only on technique that involves your grip, alignment, putting stance, posture, body position over the ball, putting stroke, and so on.

- 30 minutes: Shift your focus by spending the next 30 minutes working on distance and the feel of the greens while closely examining your putts—left to right, right to left, uphill, downhill, break patterns, and so on.

- 30 minutes: "Okay, now I'm going to work on competition." Set up some putting drills that apply the principles of competitive pressure; for example, the first putt is for par, the second putt is for a birdie, the next one's for par, and so on.

- 20 minutes: Active rest period. It's time to head into the clubhouse for a nutritious snack or a refreshing cool drink.

- Over lunch, ask yourself: "How's my technique?" "How's my feel for distance?" "How am I putting under pressure?" "How good am I at reading greens?" "How solid is my routine" and "How positive is my attitude?"

Example of a One-Week Microcycle

For a player who may compete in tournaments back to back over an extended period, here is the way a full training week might look.

Monday: Work on technical drills, revisit setup (grip, posture, and alignment), use body positions to create a better "feel." Work on technique, using implements that specifically affect mechanics. This can be a chalk line, a putting arc, or any of a variety of "tools" that are used widely. Emphasis also is placed on the specifics of the pre-putt technique and the mechanics of the setup elements. Heavy day of physical training.

Tuesday: Practice shaping shots and making notes on course conditions. Practice breathing and visualization techniques. Take the mechanical elements that were adjusted and worked on yesterday and begin the putting session with the same elements—perhaps for 15 to 20 minutes. After this, begin putting drills that emphasize both speed and locking in the repetitive motion of the adjusted and improved mechanics—perhaps 45 minutes to an hour. Medium day of physical training.

Wednesday: Pre-competition phase. Begin using new adjustments in the practice rounds. On the course, focus on ball flight and distance control and feel around the greens. Take notes on the course and prepare for the tournament. Revisit the mechanical elements—perhaps for 10 minutes or so. Thirty minutes for drills (see Tuesday). The final 45 minutes to an hour should mimic course conditions—one ball with full read and full pre-shot, finishing every missed putt. As much as possible, the player will want to get a look and feel that will be taken to the course on Thursday. Perform stretches on the course and at home with cardio work.

Thursday–Sunday: Competition. Perform daily evaluations so that you continue to learn and improve. Pre-round warm-up with putting that emphasizes mechanics and setup for approximately 5 minutes. The rest of the warm-up is congruent with on-the-course putts—one ball from various distances with full read, and so on. Finish with three to five 3-foot putts to get the look, feel, and sound of the ball going into the hole before stepping to the first tee box. Light workout and rest as needed.

Example of a Full Periodized Program for Golf

Training Phases/ Goals of Phases	Assessment/ Off-Season	Technical/ Pre-season	Pre-comp/ Pre-season	Competition	Active Rest/ Regeneration/ Off-Season
Technical	On-tee evaluation Player profile development	Motion drills (pivots, posture, grip and alignment, body motion, swing plane) Equipment fitting	Shaping shots Pre-shot routine for short game Course management	Single swing thought Part caddy/part player	Rest-reflect-evaluate
Physical	Physical assessment tests Goal setting	Super 8 strength Super 8 flexibility Body fat composition	Dynamic stretch routine Increased exercise intensity	Performance nutrition Decreased exercise intensity	Cross-training and rest
Mental	Mental assessment: confidence with clubs, attitude, on-course strategy, routine analysis	Goal setting Learn 4 P's	Pre-shot routine	One-shot-at-a-time model Post-shot routine	Rest-reflect-evaluate

Chapter 2
Elements of a Complete Golfer

The qualities that separate Tiger Woods, Ernie Els, and other champion golfers from the masses are not entirely a matter of mechanical or technical talent. Although swing mechanics and a putting stroke that holds up under pressure are important, a golfer cannot reach the limits of competitive success without two other elements: physical fitness and mental strength. Together, these are the three essential elements of being a complete golfer.

It wasn't until the early successes of Tiger Woods that we began to understand the full impact of a comprehensive training program:

Until Tiger Woods came along, I thought Jack Nicklaus was the greatest player ever. Sam Snead was the best ball striker I ever saw. . . . Ben Hogan was second with Byron Nelson pretty close to both of them. . . . But Tiger Woods, he is the complete package. He has the intelligence of Nicklaus, the guts of Arnold Palmer, the beauty of Sam's swing, the shot-making ability of Hogan, and the patience and temperament of Gandhi.

—Chi Chi Rodriquez

Comprehensive training is all about gaining the knowledge needed to adjust your game and reach your full potential as a player. Educating each player on his or her game will help that player better understand the sacrifice and dedication it takes to develop into a great golfer.

Consider the following elements in establishing a full and comprehensive training program. Although all great golfers work to develop and care for each of these eight critical areas, most golfers will find that each area overlaps or fits snuggly into one of the three main areas: technical, mental, and physical.

Keep in mind that golfers at every level are proficient in some areas while displaying weaknesses in others. Take a closer look at those areas where you are strong and those areas that have been neglected or may need more attention.

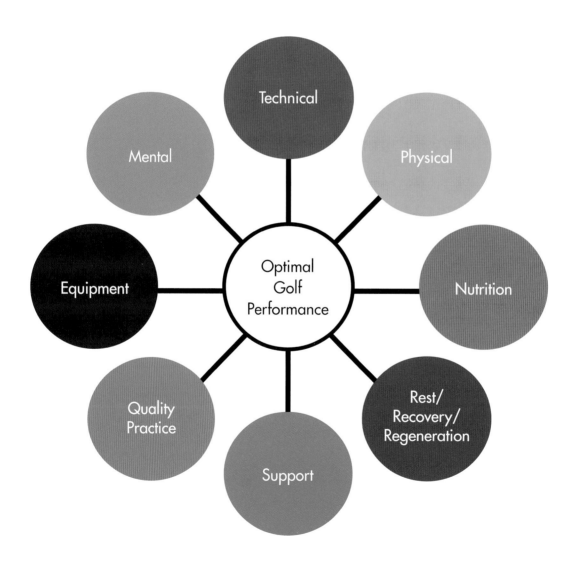

The Eight Elements

Technical

It is important to find a system or philosophy that will help you build a sound swing. Whether your personal philosophy is built on a traditional or classic swing or mimics the swing of Bobby Jones, Arnold Palmer, or Tiger Woods, it is important to embrace it as your own. Although the growing field of biomechanics has provided us with feedback on technique and perfect angle positions, many premier golfers find the swing that best reflects their body type, genetic gifts and weaknesses, and personal philosophies or those of trusted swing instructors.

Keep in mind that the golf swing is a fluid and natural movement. Some golfers base this movement on learned or practiced techniques, whereas others look for a sense of feel. In any case, it is critical to master the fundamentals. The goal is to develop a swing with these key basic ingredients: a sound grip, an athletic posture, and a synchronized backswing and downswing that will develop a solid impact position as well as a balanced follow-through.

These are the secrets that result in a dynamic golf swing, which results it consistent ball striking—which with a solid short game provides the building blocks for a player's golf career.

Whatever swing philosophy you choose, be sure to embrace it wholeheartedly and take ownership of your system or personal swing philosophy. This will help give you confidence and ultimately produce results.

Physical

As you can observe on tour, there is no single body type that is possessed by all great players. Players come in a variety of shapes and sizes, and that can be encouraging to players at all levels. In today's competitive environment, there are role models for every level of play.

Regardless of a golfer's particular body type, the majority of tour players work on their strength, stability, flexibility, mobility, nutrition, energy levels, and overall fitness. Although pioneers in the golf fitness circuit such as Gary Player and Greg Norman were among the very few who worked out and utilized the potential of fitness to their advantage, it is now widely accepted among all players that fitness is an integral part of their golf game.

Today's golfers are stronger, more powerful athletes. They train like athletes and eat like athletes. Tiger Woods may be among the most famous for his athletic body, but there are many others who are following in his footsteps. This creates competitive pressure among all high-level golfers to match his intensity and training protocols at all levels.

Golf fitness training also can provide other benefits to competitive golfers, including coping with the stress of traveling, protecting against injury, and providing longevity in competition.

Mental

Golfers can accelerate their process of development by learning how to control their emotions and accept both the good and the bad outcomes of continuous play and new experiences. Although adversity builds character, mental fortitude and patience can help any good player become more effective at the game.

More and more golfers are seeking ways to gain a competitive edge by working with sport psychologists to develop their mental games. Top players who regularly work on this aspect of their performance include Ernie Els, Retief Goosen, Tiger Woods, Annika Sörenstam, Suzann Pettersen, Davis Love III, and Brad Faxon, to name a few. For the majority of golfers who do not have access to top-ranked sports psychologists, there are a wide variety of coaches who have published their own material, which can be found at many bookstores. Players of the game today understand the need to develop their mental games to reach their full potential. Unfortunately, the golf world is full of players who are incredibly talented physically and technically but consistently fall short of their potential because of deficient mental skills.

When we start to improve our thought processes, we create feelings and emotions that in turn control our actions. Just as in developing a swing, most great players devote time and energy to learning the mental game. Through the consistent use of mental training, players can gain a competitive edge.

Nutrition

There is a strong correlation between good nutrition and playing performance. Good nutrition provides the basis for superior mental acuity and improved energy during crucial rounds. Performance nutrition for golfers includes a proper daily diet that supports the body composition and activity levels of each player. Some players need to gain muscle, and others need to lose body fat. A solid nutrition plan can accelerate the process and get a golfer to his or her goals more quickly in the off-season.

What they eat and when they eat can support golfers' performance goals or help them lose valuable strokes on their scorecards. Golfers can find themselves on the course for many long stretches during long hours of practice and additional hours of play. This is where a well-thought-out nutrition plan can make the difference between one player and the next on the leader board.

Rest, Recovery, and Regeneration

This is an area that is overlooked by athletes at all levels. Although the commitment to working hard is important, it must be matched by the commitment to rest, recover, and allow the body to regenerate.

Research has indicated that one of the major reasons highly skilled athletes do not perform up to their ability at major competitions is that they are not well rested. Maintaining balance in your life is critical to your development as a person. Having hobbies and other interests will help you reflect on your mission and recharge your batteries. It is important to develop relationships and keep golf in perspective. This will help you draw from your life experiences and cope with new challenges in the future. A balanced lifestyle will help you reach your goals faster and keep you mentally strong through challenges and throughout your golfing career.

Support System

It can be difficult to achieve your goals without having a solid support network. If your goal is to strive for excellence, support from your family, friends, and coaches can be instrumental. Surrounding yourself with a strong support network can be nourishing to your spirit and uplifting to you as a player.

Watch PGA tournament endings when players such as Phil Mickelson and Tiger Woods secure a big win. Often you see Phil's wife and daughters rush up to greet him with a big hug and congratulations. When Tiger's dad was alive and healthy, you always saw his parents at his side, supporting his competitive spirit.

When your desire is to be more successful, it helps to surround yourself with those who support your goals and dreams instead of those who distract you. A solid support system can help hold you accountable and keep you focused when you need it most.

Quality Practice

Quality practice habits promote quality play. It is common knowledge that many golfers struggle with taking their practice performance from the range to the course. One of the reasons for this is that they fail to practice in conditions that resemble competitive play. Remember, the goal of practicing is to become a better player, not a better practicer. One of the easiest ways to see better results on the course is to practice with a purpose. This purpose is a dedicated, well-thought-out plan with a specific goal in mind. Golfers report that they get the best results by changing clubs and targets frequently, shaping shots, and sticking to a solid routine.

Equipment

Well-fitted equipment can have an immediate impact on your performance. Although there are a wide variety of choices with regard to selecting the right equipment, an experienced club fitter can help you select the correct shaft length, flex, and weight.

The appropriate weight of the head combined with the correct shaft length will give you the desired swing weight. Grips should be the right size to allow your hands to sit correctly on the club. The correct lies and lofts will assist you with the type of shot pattern you are trying to create. Take advantage of advances in club manufacturing and ball construction to get the most out of your body, your skill set, and your game.

Understanding your strengths and weaknesses as a player will dictate the types of clubs you carry in the bag. For many women and high-handicap men, using lofted woods or hybrid clubs rather than the full complement of traditional irons can shave strokes off the scorecard, as these clubs are typically more forgiving, particularly out of the rough. Also, many of the mid- to low-handicap players may benefit by playing with an extra wedge in the bag to accommodate the myriad of shots around the green in the "scoring area" within 100 yards of the hole. Experimenting with a variety of clubs, lofts, and wedges has had a profound positive impact on many players' games. However, make sure that once a good mix is found, you don't change clubs just for change's sake! Many golfers think that the latest club they see their favorite tour pro using must be the best for them as well. When you get the swing mechanics, swing speed, and physique of a tour player, you can consider adjusting to that type of equipment!

The Winning Attitude

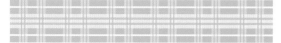

Achieving peak performance involves all eight controllable factors with the important addition of a winning attitude. To make significant improvements in your game, you must believe that you can! One of the few things that you as a golfer can control completely with regard to your game of golf is your attitude. Wind, rain, poor lies, and golfing partners who play slowly or talk too much can be frustrating and are outside your control. Players who learn to shut out those distractions and have a winning attitude provide themselves the best chance to play at their peak level. Below are the characteristics that typify the attitude of a winning golfer:

- **As a winner, you believe in yourself**: Without a strong belief in your ability to execute shots, you consistently will doubt yourself on the golf course. Practicing enough that you have confidence on your game and then going out on the course with the belief that you're capable of playing well is an important component of a winning attitude.

- **Winners accept challenges enthusiastically**: When faced with difficult situations, most players look at them in a negative light: "Oh, just my luck. I hit a great drive, and it lands in a divot" or "I can't believe that the ball is buried so deeply in the bunker."

The great players in the game accept these situations as a natural, "everyday" part of the game and approach these circumstances with enthusiasm. They understand that focusing on the solution instead of the problem is the key to becoming a better golfer, and they know that working their way out of trouble helps them become stronger players over time.

- **Winning golfers work hard and persevere**: What does working hard mean to you? To a golfer who is serious about the game, this means doing whatever it takes to become the best player one can be. If extra putting practice is called for, you see this player on the putting green. When the irons are shaky, you see this player hitting extra balls at the range. When it is necessary to scale back on training because the player is overtired, this player takes time off to rest and recover. Perseverance refers to the player continuing to give effort no matter what the obstacles are.

- **Winners make the most of their natural talents**: A smart golfer with a winning attitude plays within his or her strengths. This includes working diligently to improve one's weaknesses as well. The desired result here is to reach your ultimate potential. Achieving this requires that you give due consideration to genetic, time, and money constraints while taking advantage of the opportunities that come your way. Become the best golfer you can be.

- **Winners stay focused on their goals**: This winning attitude is essential for a serious golfer at every level. First, a player must identify his or her goal. It is difficult to know if you are on the right road if you don't know your destination! Once this has been defined clearly, structure your practice and play with this ultimate goal in mind. No single shot, no hole, no round of golf is as important as the goal you're

attempting to achieve. Everything that you undertake in golf is done with this purpose in mind. A lot of golfers beat balls around with little purpose. Winning golfers have a purpose for nearly everything they do that is related to golf.

- **Winners take responsibility**: There are a million excuses that most golfers use for not achieving what they want to achieve. A golfer with a winning attitude takes responsibility for his or her development as a player and offers no excuses along the path to success. Rather than trying to figure out whose fault it is that something went wrong, put more energy into finding alternative methods to achieve the success you seek. Make your own choices about your game. Ultimately you will learn lessons from poor choices and earn benefits from good choices.

- **Winning golfers keep it all in perspective**: A winner doesn't let himself get too excited over victories or too inconsolable over defeats. While wanting to win, a winner typically doesn't feel as though she "has to" win in order to be "okay." Your winning attitude involves maintaining a sense of humor toward yourself and the game—no matter how challenging or frustrating it may be.

- **Winners are flexible**: Adaptability is the last characteristic of a winning attitude. Once a winner chooses his path, he understands that there are going to be deviations along the way. A pilot flying an airplane between two cities sometimes may have to go higher or lower because of the weather or air traffic or may take a route that isn't a straight line because another route is safer for the passengers. A winner also keeps the destination in mind while remaining flexible and making adjustments when encountering things over which he has little control.

Chapter 3

Assess Your Game

The real work begins here as the golfer makes an honest assessment of the strengths and weaknesses of his entire game. Although this can be a difficult exercise at times, it also can be fun. The assessment phase engages a golfer's mind, allowing him to think clearly about where he stands and where he wants to go. Often, the result is a more positive outlook on his game than he might have expected, building confidence for the long process ahead.

Assessments represent a significant amount of work on the part of the reader, but they are exercises that can be fun and enjoyable. The purpose of this book is to help readers learn about themselves and better their golf games, and these assessments provide a huge jump start to that process.

Understanding the Destination

"Ladies and gentlemen, this is your flight attendant speaking. I'd like to welcome you and thank you for flying with us today. Our pilot has just informed me that she has no idea of our final destination. Additionally, in the event of any unforeseen trouble along the way, she has no alternative plan for corrective action . . ."

Would you be interested in being a passenger on this flight? We didn't think so. The reality, however, is that this probably resembles your past attempts at improving your golf game—no plan, no specific destination in mind, and little awareness of when you're headed "off-course."

There are no shortcuts to true improvement, just as there are no shortcuts for a pilot going from Los Angeles to New York. No matter how she might try, the pilot still has to cross the whole country. But if you honestly assess your game and map out a process of improvement, you will get there. It will take more work initially, but it's better than hitting ball after ball on the driving range, year after year, and not seeing your handicap go down.

Golf gives you the opportunity to analyze every detail and component of your game—technical, physical, and mental. From these initial assessments, you can set short- and long-term goals and form an action plan. This is exactly what great golfers do when they are attempting to improve. Just like them, you will be able to identify which phase of training you are in and what you are working on physically, technically,

or mentally. This plan will help you overcome obstacles and reach your peak performance.

Commit to undergoing a full game assessment at the end of your peak golf season. This is the natural time to take a look back and reflect on what you did right (a lot, let's hope) and what needs to be adjusted. For tour pros, this phase usually begins in November and extends into the early part of the next year—about an 8-week program. For most of you, weather, school, or family commitments probably will dictate the boundaries of your "off-season."

If you are training for a specific competitive goal, simply set aside an appropriate amount of time to perform the assessments. For example, if your goal is to win a club championship in mid-August, you may want to set aside time for assessments when you are 6 to 8 weeks away from the first day of the big event. In this chapter, you'll learn how to assess your game properly and get started on an action plan for improvement.

Technical Evaluations

The Makings of a Champion

To perform like a champion, it helps to study the success of those we call champions. In golf, Tiger Woods is most worthy of study, based on his comprehensive training methods, unbridled level of energy and passion for the game, superb mental focus, and physical fitness. Through education and observation, you will be able to understand the sacrifice and dedication it takes to develop into a great golfer and face adversity as you go through the inevitable bumps along the road. Begin this process with an assessment of your own game in as much detail as possible.

The quickest way to build your golf swing is through the use of drills and teaching aids. Extensive video analysis and mental imagery will help accelerate the process. This will give you the feel and the necessary feedback to produce the correct movements in your swing. You will need a clear understanding of the basics, as they provide the foundation for your game. An example of a basic is that the arms and upper body control the movement of the lower body. Your goal is to develop a swing with these key ingredients: a sound grip, an athletic posture, a synchronized backswing and downswing, a solid impact position, and a balanced follow-through. The goal in this technical assessment phase is to improve your mechanics and become a better player.

Boring Statistics Can Make You a Better Player

Some golfers gravitate more naturally to numbers and statistics than others do. No matter which side you fall on, take a cue from tour players, most of whom know how many fairways they hit each round, how many greens they reach in regulation, their up and down percentages, and their number of putts per round. Isn't this a case of paralysis by analysis? you ask. No. With this knowledge, the pros plan their practice sessions around one goal: improving their weakest areas. Like them, you will shoot lower scores when you become consistent in all areas of the game. Sure, it's more fun to hit shots you already can perform with ease, but it's more productive to work on improving your weaknesses.

With that in mind, keep statistics for every round you play. You will learn where you need to improve and be able to plan your practice sessions accordingly. Follow this advice and watch your scores go down!

On-Tee Evaluation

You should start the assessment process with an "on-tee evaluation," which serves to identify specific areas where you will take corrective action in the technical phase. Make a copy of the form on page 29 and take it to the course. Be honest in your evaluation. The more information you can gather from your round, the better equipped you will be to make changes.

Note: More experienced players often are able to rate themselves easily, as they play more often and are in tune with their games. Less experienced players should play three rounds, take notes, and then fill out this form.

On-Tee Evaluation Form

Date: _____

Name: _____

Ratings:
Excellent = 1
Very good = 2
Average = 3
Fair = 4
Poor = 5

Putting	Chipping	Alignment
_____ 1. Long putts	_____ 1. Long, running chips	_____ 1. Shoulders
_____ 2. Short putts	_____ 2. Short chips	_____ 2. Hips
_____ 3. Right to left	_____ 3. Chips from rough	_____ 3. Knees
_____ 4. Left to right	_____ 4. Distance control	_____ 4. Feet
_____ 5. Downhill	_____ 5. Recovery from bad lies	_____ 5. Club face
_____ 6. Uphill	_____ 6. Setup	_____ 6. Ball position
_____ 7. Distance control		_____ 7. Eye line
_____ 8. Setup		_____ OVERALL ALIGNMENT

Bunker Play	Iron Play	Grip
_____ 1. Setup	_____ 1. Short irons	_____ 1. Left hand
_____ 2. Feel	_____ 2. Midirons	_____ 2. Right hand
_____ 3. Uphill lies	_____ 3. Long irons	_____ 3. Grip pressure
_____ 4. Downhill lies	_____ 4. Shaping shots	_____ 4. Clubface
_____ 5. Sidehill lies	_____ 5. Trajectory control	
_____ 6. Fairway bunkers	_____ 6. Distance control	

Woods	Pitching	Setup
_____ 1. Driver	_____ 1. Setup	_____ 1. Posture
_____ 2. Fairway woods	_____ 2. Distance control	_____ 2. Knee flex
_____ 3. Accuracy	_____ 3. Low pitches	_____ 3. Spine tilt
_____ 4. Power	_____ 4. High pitches	_____ 4. Weight distribution
_____ 5. Setup	_____ 5. Recovery shots	_____ 5. Stance width

The most important thing after filling out an on-tee evaluation is not to get discouraged. Even champion golfers must work on some aspects of their game. From 2002 through 2004, Gary Gilchrist worked with Michelle Wie as her primary swing instructor. As part of her development process, Michelle filled out the exact same evaluation form you just completed. Based on her ratings, here is an actual profile created during Michelle's assessment period:

Player Development Profile
STUDENT: Michelle Wie
COACH: Gary Gilchrist
DATES: March 18–21, 2003;
March 25–28, 2003

Tournaments: Safeway International and Nabisco Dinah Shore

Strengths and limitations: Michelle has the ability to adapt quickly to tournament conditions. Still needs time to build her strength and endurance for an entire week of golf.

Overall Instructional Profile
Grip: Right-hand grip sometimes gets on top. Rotate away from target for a stronger right-hand grip.

Posture: Top-heavy, leans too far over. Use posture drill to get her weight more underneath her.

Alignment: Clubface points right. Goal at address is to square the face.

Pivot: Too much head movement off the ball. Work on pivot drills, feeling the weight moving laterally into the left toe and then behind it. This will slow down the hips.

Takeaway: Butt end of club moves out away from her. Too much right-arm rotation. Fix by moving the club with the body so that the clubhead stays outside her hands.

Backswing: Elbows stay too close together. Too much head movement in her body motion. Fix when setting the club; feel wider elbows and the club more over her right shoulder.

Downswing: Left side clears too early. Right hip and knee move out early, and club then lags behind. Fix: Improve backswing; this will help the club naturally get more shallow. Feel her weight moving onto her left toe and hold her right hip back.

Impact: Right side lifts up and out because her left side clears too early.

Follow-through: Swings too much "in to out." Fix: Backswing needs to be more in front; on the downswing the club will shallow out, with her body moving more laterally. Hands should move left and up. Make more of a body release.

Swing tempo/rhythm: Sometimes swings quick under pressure.

> ### Drills
> 1. Swing in a bunker.
> 2. Multiple feet-together and right-foot-back repetitions.
> 3. Make a full swing, then swing halfway, stop, and check the turn to the top. Then continue through, feeling the right weight transfer.

Long Game

Short irons: Tempo with these helps improve full swing with longer clubs.

Midirons: Feel three-quarter swings.

Long irons: Tempo was good.

Driver: Focus on a one-piece takeaway.

Fairway woods: Great!

Short Game

Putting: Posture eye line is slightly inside the ball. Club shaft angle at 90 degrees; close right eye to check on this. Keep head still throughout the stroke. The goal is to listen to the ball falling into the cup rather than look at it.

Chipping: Keep head still; backswing straighter back.

Pitching: Good work on tempo. Backswing sometimes too far inside, and follow-through gets too long.

Lob shots: Good. The continued key is a light grip pressure.

Bunker shots: On the backswing, take club along her body line. On the downswing, move the club down her target line.

Fairway bunkers: Clubface open; weight left; choose one more club and swing at 80 percent with no release of the hands.

This assessment makes it clear that Michelle has a lot to work on, and that is not unusual for top-level players. Whether you are a recreational golfer who longs to play better golf or a player like Michelle Wie, the process of a complete game assessment is necessary to reach your full playing potential.

Mental Game Evaluations

Perception versus Reality

Frequently, when we ask players about their goals, their response is "to get better." But what does that mean? Better at what? How will you measure it? What is your plan to make this happen? The mental game evaluations will help you determine the answers to these questions. Although a high level of focus, intensity, and specificity may not seem applicable if you are not interested in high-level tournament competition, the truth is that a strong mental focus is just as effective and helpful for you as it is for elite players.

Without immediate access to a "mental guru," you must rely on self-evaluation and input from trusted people in your golf world. Swing instructors, frequent playing partners, parents, and teammates all can give you insight into how they see your mental game. The idea here is not that anyone's information is the objective truth, but experience shows that many players have blind spots in regard to where they are strong or weak. Getting insight from others will help you compare and contrast the way you see your game with the way others see it.

Create an Action Plan

Golfers know that it is perfectly acceptable to complain and pontificate about how poorly they play. Listen to the discussions around the typical nineteenth hole at any golf course in the country. Frequently, golfers are speaking about the components of their game that don't work very well: "I couldn't make a putt today," "I can't hit my driver for the life of me," "I don't know if I'll ever be able to play out of the sand." If this sounds like you, you need an action plan for improving your mental game. However, as with many things in life, it is far easier to contemplate changing one's attitude than to take the necessary steps to get it done.

Thinking and complaining isn't taking action. Even for those of you who can't or won't take the time to practice your swings regularly, working on even one component of your mental game can be of tremendous benefit.

You will see that doing something about the deficiencies in your mental game will give you a real sense that you are working toward making a positive change. In and of itself, that can increase your confidence on the course and affect your swing mechanics.

Gather information about your mental game and then prioritize the areas on which you want to work. Most people work much more diligently when they face a deadline, and this "positive pressure" may be what it takes to keep you moving in the right direction. Simply work the priorities into your normal golf routine for the very best results.

Use the form on page 34 to make a commitment to a plan and to schedule your week accordingly. Then watch as your actions translate into greater proficiency in the areas you've identified as concerns.

Filling out an evaluation form such as this can provide a wealth of information. Perhaps you tend to get ahead of yourself rather than focus on the shot at hand, or maybe you have difficulty reigning in your negative emotions after you hit a poor shot. Whatever may apply in your case, you can take steps during the assessment phase to prepare yourself for the hard work ahead.

Focus/Confidence Evaluation Form

Date: _____

Name: _____

Preparation	On-Course Focus	On-Course Strategy
_____1. Practice day plan	_____1. Concentration	_____1. Use of yardage book
_____2. Pre-round attitude	_____2. Effort	_____2. Choosing a target
_____3. Pre-shot routine	_____3. Self-talk	_____3. Picking the best target
_____4. Pre-putt routine	_____4. Imagination	_____4. Playing one shot at a time
_____OVERALL PREPARATION	_____5. Time management	_____5. Club selection
	_____OVERALL ON-COURSE	_____6. Post-round analysis
		_____OVERALL STRATEGY

Rate your confidence with each of your clubs (10 = highest, 1 = lowest):		
_____Driver	_____3 iron	_____8 iron
_____3 wood	_____4 iron	_____9 iron
_____5 wood	_____5 iron	_____Pitching wedge
_____Hybrid	_____6 iron	_____Sand wedge
_____Putter	_____7 iron	_____Lob wedge

Here are some observations you should be making as part of your self-evaluation:

- Which clubs are you most/least confident with?

- How do handle pressure and stress when playing?

- Are you able to stay focused from one shot to the next?

- What inconsistencies have you noticed when playing? Do you begin optimistic and end pessimistic? Does your attitude change from one shot to the next or one hole to the next?

- Do you tend to play it safe or take risks? Does your level of aggression change during the round? What factors cause it to change?

- Do you need more imagination when attempting to visualize potential shots?

- When faced with course hazards such as water and sand, do you find it more visually distracting when the hazard is to your left, your right, or directly in front of your line?

- Are you able to control your distance the way you want? Does your control change from woods to short irons or with other club variations?

- How are you at reading greens? Do you read better on uphill or downhill lies?

As you can see, there are a myriad of opportunities to assess your mental game tendencies. Although this may seem like overkill at first, it provides vital data with which to make critical decisions regarding your game. As you get to know yourself and your playing traits better, the process will become simpler so that you can know when and how to get back on track more quickly.

Accurate evaluation involves the sometimes difficult task of being brutally honest with yourself. There are times when some of us are not completely truthful—even with ourselves. We sometimes will not accept feedback that comes from others or feedback that comes from our own observations. There are times we won't accept criticism, and there are times we won't accept praise. It is important to be open to both praise and criticism and to get the most comprehensive and thorough feedback possible about your game from a wide variety of sources.

How to Play Your Own Game

It can be difficult to understand and appreciate your own game if you constantly compare yourself to other people. This is natural. We do it at home, in our social circles, and on the golf course.

However, when people begin analyzing themselves, certain attributes inevitably leave them feeling insecure: "I'm shorter than everyone," "I'm taller than everyone," "I'm skinnier than everyone," "I'm heavier than everyone." This type of thinking creates additional insecurities about the game: "I can't hit it as far as most kids," "I don't putt as well as he does," "We don't have as much money, so I don't get the instruction that she does."

Insecurities make it difficult to "play your own game." Instead of trying to play to their own strengths, players often try to be someone they are not, try to keep up with what others are doing, or try to do things that are not in their capacity. Focusing on what others are doing can hurt a player's confidence, and it also regularly affects the player's course management decisions. These are among the more common mistakes:

- Unconsciously pulling the driver out of the bag in order to hit the ball as far off the tee as possible

- Automatically pulling a 3 wood for the second shot into a par 5

- Consistently "underclubbing" by falsely believing certain clubs hit farther than they actually do

- Making high-risk/low-reward shot selection decisions

- Swinging the club harder to try to hit the ball farther

The best way to fight your insecurities is to be honest and objective about the strengths and capabilities you bring to the course as a player. This is what is referred to as "playing within yourself." When you recognize and acknowledge your strengths, you will begin to play the game in the way that is best for you rather than mimicking what others are doing or playing the way you think the game should be played. When we judge ourselves against others, whether in life or in golf, we will always find someone who is better at something than we are.

It is hard to get your ego out of the way and play shorter or lay up when your competitor can get there in two strokes. It is difficult emotionally to hit a 5 iron to a par-3 hole when your competitor hits a 9 iron. It is a challenge to continue doing what you're doing if you see a competitor who is successful doing something different.

People who constantly follow others lose the sense of who they really are. In golf, players who are distracted by others often get lost because

they are changing their game constantly. Be like the best players in the world. The most successful golfers of any age figure out what they're good at, understand what works for them, and then make a commitment to focus on their strengths.

Physical Assessments and Evaluations

The Golf Fitness Frontier

If you are stronger or more flexible, you will play better golf, right? Well, not exactly. In elite golf fitness training, we take it a step further by studying the biomechanics of the swing and an individual player's movement patterns, looking for inefficiencies. These inefficiencies often lead to swing faults and difficulties getting the body into the various positions needed for a more varied number of shot selections. David Leadbetter says that a "good swing motion results from a chain reaction of good positions." Being in poor physical condition interrupts that chain reaction.

Two-time U.S. Open champion Lee Janzen, age 43 at that time, was asked what percentage of golfers on the tour use fitness training to play better golf. His answer was very revealing: "I would think it would be easier to find the guys that aren't working out. I think it's probably just a handful of guys that are not doing some sort of exercise. Even the guys that don't look like they're in shape, I do see them go into the trailer and work out and stretch. They are making an effort to at least get stronger or maybe eliminate the risk of injury by getting in better shape."

Competitive golfers understand that fitness is a vital component of their overall success. Here's what some of the world's best golfers have said about fitness and its effect on their golf games:

A lot of what I've been able to accomplish in golf is the direct result of becoming physically stronger.

—*Tiger Woods*

I've worked so hard with my golf swing through the years. Once your golf swing comes to a point where you can't improve it anymore, all you do is just repeat it. My workout kind of elevated that. I'm much stronger with the shots I'm hitting. I'm driving the ball farther than I ever have, which tells you something. My trainer has done great work with me.

—*Vijay Singh*

I practice less golf, and I spend more time in the gym. I know that if my body is in good shape, I'll be able to swing the club the way I want to.

—*Annika Sörenstam*

Lessons from the Trainers of the Pros

If it's good enough for Annika, it's good enough for you! In training, we always want to train and teach for the best and let the players decide how much time, interest, and energy they want to put into their game. There are ways to perform "good," "better," and "best" exercise programs. In most cases, your enthusiasm and the time invested will be reflected in lower scores.

During the 2002–2003 off-season, Annika Sörenstam made big news when in a self-assessment of her game she determined that her weakness in driving distance was a result of her lack of core strength and stability. According to her trainer, Kai Fusser, "When we started, she put the clubs away for about eight weeks. She didn't touch her clubs; she didn't hit any balls. We started in November, and when her coach saw her in the middle of January, he noticed that she probably gained ten yards in the first two months. She was also much more receptive to swing instruction. He would ask her to perform a certain movement, and because of her increased fitness it was a lot easier for her to repeat that. She got back to the top level of her game within a few days, whereas it normally would take a few weeks."

Compute Your Golf Fitness Score

Although it is only natural to look in the mirror and assess your fitness visually, it is more effective to go through a series of flexibility, strength, balance, and stamina tests. When we put our students through these tests, we see stark differences from player to player even if outwardly they seem to be in similar physical shape. Some golfers have amazing flexibility but lack muscle strength. Others lose all their energy on the back nine because of poor conditioning. Or maybe a golfer also bikes, hikes, or runs and has the heart capacity of a champion yet can't touch his toes or make a full backswing as a result of poor flexibility in his shoulders. The only way to find out which category you fit in and how to go about improving your physical fitness is to go through this battery of tests. Here are a few areas of significance that the tests touch on:

1. Flexibility. The "big three" in the area of flexibility are hip rotation, spine rotation, and shoulder rotation. When you lack a full range of motion in any of these key areas, inconsistencies begin to appear in your swing. For example, if you have limited right hip rotation, you may have a lateral sway in your backswing to compensate. Your mechanics also break down if you are unable to complete a full range of motion. We have seen golfers with tremendous flexibility in their upper bodies yet significant restrictions in their lower bodies. Too much of one type of range of motion does not make up for a deficit in another. They must complement each other for the swing to work properly.

2. Strength. This is the area where we see the biggest discrepancies, even in the same golfer. Some players have strong upper bodies but lack lower-body strength; others are the opposite. As you move forward with strength training, think in terms of whole-body strength and how and where it is derived. Try to get away from compartmentalized training of single muscles. At no point in the swing is just one muscle activated. There is great synergy between many muscle groups and the way they function together. Here is a phrase used to explain how to train for golf: Work on your "go" muscles, not your "show" muscles. In other words, use exercises that train for your movement pattern, not just the muscles you see in the mirror.

3. Stability. The golf swing is a dynamic athletic motion. As such, it demands stability—your ankles can't be moving in one direction while your knees move in another. We see golfers at all handicap levels feel challenged by their stability. If you are having trouble stabilizing yourself through your swing and often fall off balance, you need to seek ways to eliminate extra uncontrolled movements that detract from your stability.

Making an accurate assessment of your current physical fitness level will help you notice differences in your body in terms of stability, strength, and flexibility. Once you have that information, you can prioritize your fitness needs going forward and create a more efficient swing. The following are 10 self-tests. Go through them all and give yourself point values on the basis of what you see your body doing. You then can use those points to compute your golf fitness score. Be sure to notice subtle differences in your right side versus your left side and your upper body versus your lower body. These kinds of muscle imbalances can wreak havoc on your golf swing.

Golf Fitness Test 1: Deep Squat

Squat Starting Position

1. Place each of your hands on the opposite ends of a golf club, with your hands slightly more than shoulder width apart.

2. Spread your feet to about shoulder width apart.

Correct Full Squat Position

1. Slowly proceed to a full squat position while extending your arms into the air, above your head.

2. Sit as far down as comfortably as possible while keeping your heels in contact with the ground.

3. Maintain proper golf posture throughout the movement.

- If you experience a loss of spine angle, balance, and heel contact with the floor or have knee alignment that extends past your toes, **give yourself 1 point.**

- If you lose some spine angle and can maintain some heel contact while being able to complete a nearly full squat, **give yourself 2 points.**

- If your thighs reach parallel or greater, your heels maintain contact with the floor, your knees stay in alignment, and your spine angle remains the same, **you've earned 3 points.**

Golf Fitness Test 2: Core Engagement

Stance with String around Waist

1. Cut a string long enough to tie around your waist and stand upright.

2. Tie the string around your waist so that it is taut (somewhat tight).

Bending Position

Place an object in front of you and then bend down and pick up the object.

Repeat this test a few times and score yourself on the basis of what typically happens to the string when you bend down:

- If the string feels tighter around your midsection, **give yourself 1 point.**

- If the string feels the same as it did before you bent down, **give yourself 2 points.**

- If the string feels looser around your torso, **give yourself 3 points.**

Golf Fitness Test 3: Golfer's Core Endurance

Raised Push-Up Position

1. Lie facedown in a push-up position with your elbows directly beneath your shoulders.

2. Push off with your feet and elbows to raise your body into the air.

3. Your body should form one line from the ears to the heels.

4. Hold this position as long as you can without feeling any pain or discomfort in the lower back.

How long were you able to hold this position (without altering your posture or body position)?

- 45 seconds or less, **give yourself 1 point.**
- 45 seconds to 1 minute, **take 2 points.**
- Over 1 minute, **you deserve 3 points.**

Golf Fitness Test 4: Golfer's Seated Rotation

Starting Position

1. Sit on an inflatable exercise ball or a chair, using good posture (back straight up and down).

2. Place your feet about shoulder width apart and look straight ahead.

3. Place a long iron or 3 wood behind your shoulders and hold each end with your hands.

Midrotation

1. Rotate to your left as far as possible and then to your right.

2. Be sure your hips do not rotate along with your shoulders.

Full Rotation

Make note of where the middle of your chest (not your head) is facing as you reach maximum rotation.

Notice the final resting place of the middle of your chest in full rotation to your left. Assign the following point values depending on where your chest points when it rotates:

- If you can point your chest only as far as your left leg or less than 30 degrees, **give yourself 1 point.**

- If you can point your chest past your left leg and up 45 degrees, **give yourself 2 points.**

- If you can rotate up to a full 90 degrees, **give yourself 3 points.**

Golf Fitness Test 5: Standing Dynamic Balance

Starting Position

Start in an athletic golf posture and fold both hands across your chest.

Foot Lifted

If you are right-handed, move your right foot behind you and off the ground several inches. If you are left-handed, keep your right foot on the ground and do this with the left foot.

Lift and Rotate

Keeping your hands on your chest, rotate to a "backswing," then "follow-through" position. Notice what is happening with your balance and knee and hip movement.

- If your knees and/or ankles are moving rapidly and you are off balance, **give yourself 1 point.**

- If you have excessive movement at either the knee or the ankle, **give yourself 2 points.**

- If you maintained your balance and have very minimal movement at your ankles and knees, **give yourself 3 points.**

Golf Fitness Test 6: Shoulder Mobility and Flexibility

Reaching Behind Back

1. From a standing position, take your left hand and reach behind your back toward the opposite shoulder blade.

2. Now reach over the right shoulder and toward the left shoulder blade.

3. Note the final resting position of your fingertips. Can your hands touch from behind your back?

- If you couldn't touch your hands anywhere near your opposite shoulder blades, **give yourself 1 point.**

- If you could nearly reach your opposite shoulder blades, **give yourself 2 points.**

- If you could comfortably reach both opposite shoulder blades and touch your hands from behind your back, **give yourself 3 points.**

Golf Fitness Test 7: Upper-Body Strength

Push-Up Starting Position

1. Men should perform standard push-ups; women should perform modified push-ups with the knees touching the floor.

2. For standard push-ups, only the hands and feet should be in contact with the floor.

Lowered Push-Up Position

1. Lower your body to within one fist height of the floor.

2. Rest is allowed only in the "up" position.

3. Perform as many push-ups as possible until fatigue stops you from completing one more.

- If you can do 5 or fewer push-ups, **give yourself 1 point.**

- If you can do 6 to 12 push-ups, **give yourself 2 points.**

- If you can do more than 13 push-ups, **give yourself 3 points.**

Golf Fitness Test 8: Static Balance

Starting Position, Palms Out

Stand on a hard surface.

Foot Lifted, Eyes Closed

1. Close your eyes and lift one foot about 6 inches off the ground. Your knee will be bent at about a 45-degree angle.

2. Place your arms at your hips or resting at your sides.

3. Have someone record how long you are able to hold this position without swaying from side to side or resting your knee against the supporting leg.

- If you can hold this position for less than 10 seconds, **give yourself 1 point.**

- If you can hold this position for 11 to 20 seconds, **give yourself 2 points.**

- If you can hold this position for more than 20 seconds, **give yourself 3 points.**

Golf Fitness Test 9: Hip Mobility/Flexibility

Starting Position against Wall

Stand with your back against a wall and your feet about hip width apart.

Rotated Heel

1. Slowly rotate the right heel outward and then do the same thing with the left heel.

2. Be sure that your leg is straight and that you don't move your hips from a square position against the wall.

3. Notice how far you were able to rotate your heels.

- If you rotated your heel out slightly, **give yourself 1 point.**

- If you rotated your heel out to 45 degrees, **give yourself 2 points.**

- If you rotated your heel past 45 degrees, **give yourself 3 points.**

Golf Fitness Test 10: Lower-Body Strength

Starting Position against Wall

Place your back firmly against a wall with your feet shoulder width apart and parallel.

Flexed Wall Squat

1. Slide down along the wall until your knees are flexed to 90 degrees.

2. Make sure the knees do not extend over the top of the feet (don't go past 90 degrees). Try to push against the wall with the small of your back against the wall.

3. Record the number of seconds you are able to hold this position.

- If you were able to maintain this position against the wall for 1 minute or less, **give yourself 1 point.**

- If you were able to maintain this position against the wall between 1 and 1¹⁄₂ minutes, **give yourself 2 points.**

- If you were able to stay against the wall for 2 minutes or longer, **award yourself 3 points.**

Golf Fitness Score Breakdown

25 to 30 points: You have a high degree of golf fitness and should continue the training methods you have been using or perhaps begin challenging yourself with a new level.

20 to 25 points: It's time to begin working on exercises and stretches that speak to your areas of weakness. Those areas may be holding you back from reaching your potential.

20 points or below: It's time to get to work! A stretching and strengthening program will provide immediate benefits to your game.

Swing Fault Identification

If you are in either of the lower score categories, you probably have swing faults that are caused by a lack of golf-specific fitness. Common faults include the following:

- An inability to transfer weight to your right side in the backswing and/or to your left side in the downswing

- Insufficient rotation of the hips both back and through

- Loss of balance during or after the downswing

- Inconsistent posture (lifting the upper body during the swing)

- Inability to get enough separation between your shoulder and hip rotation

- Excessive rolling of the feet during the downswing

- Difficulty maintaining a firm grip on the club at impact

If any of these descriptions sound like you, you're not alone! Don't get discouraged, because physical fitness is something that anyone can improve. Your focus in golf training should be on the postural muscles that provide support during the swing from the address to the finish. This part of the regimen will not be easy, and you may be tempted to throw in the towel and look for other ways to solve your swing faults. But that is not the answer. By sticking to an intense fitness program, you soon will reap the benefits of a body that can handle the golf swing you want.

Get Your Body "Golf-Ready"

We've just seen how important flexibility, strength, and stability are to building a great golf swing, but what about some of the more basic components of human health, such as body fat and cardiovascular health? It is fair to assume that the "beer belly" seen in golf clubhouses around the nation not only jeopardizes a golfer's health but also affects his ability to make the type of golf swing that he has the talent to perform.

Many questions arise regarding the safe and effective body fat percentages required to play one's best golf. As Tiger Woods once said, "I would never want to lose a tournament precipitated by my being out of shape." Here is a table of healthy body fat percentages:

Age	Up to 30	30–50	50+
Females	14–21%	15–23%	16–25%
Males	9–15%	11–17%	12–19%

Sport	Male	Female	Sport	Male	Female
Baseball	12–15%	12–18%	Rowing	6–14%	12–18%
Basketball	6–12%	20–27%	Shot putting	16–20%	20–28%
Body building	5–8%	10–15%	Cross-country skiing	7–12%	16–22%
Cycling	5–15%	15–20%	Sprinting	8–10%	12–20%
Football (backs)	9–12%	No data	Swimming	9–12%	14–24%
Football (linemen)	15–19%	No data	Tennis	12–16%	16–24%
Gymnastics	5–12%	10–16%	Triathlon	5–12%	10–15%
High/long jumping	7–12%	10–18%	Volleyball	11–14%	16–25%
Ice/field hockey	8–15%	12–18%	Weightlifting	9–16%	No data
Racquetball	8–13%	15–22%	Wrestling	5–16%	No data

You'll notice that golf is not on this list; that's the case because it's such a recent phenomenon to have professional golfers monitoring their physical fitness. Does anyone really know about the fitness levels of two of the world's best golfers, Tiger Woods and Annika Sörenstam?

In a September 2001 article in *Golf Digest*, Tiger Woods exclaimed:

I work my butt off to maintain physical fitness, but I also try to eat right. The combination has helped me increase my overall strength and that, probably more than anything, is the reason I've been able to take my game to the next level. My body fat is somewhere around 5 percent. To get there I had to cut back on empty calories (non-nutritional foods like fried chicken and pizza). I still love the occasional cheeseburger, and I'm a sucker for Mom's sticky rice and mangoes, but I no longer pig out on them. I prefer leaner cuts of meat, cereals and egg-white omelets. My goal is to remain healthy my entire career, and a healthy diet seems like a good start.

According to Rob Schumacher in an article written for the *Arizona Republic*, "How tough is Sörenstam? About as tough as they come, says her personal trainer, Kai Fusser. Sörenstam enjoyed a career year in 2001, winning eight tournaments, her fourth Rolex Player of the Year award and the money title in a season she fired a 59. But she wasn't satisfied. She had a swing coach, but in the off-season hired Fusser as her 'body coach.' When she first began working out with Fusser, she couldn't perform one pull-up. Now she routinely does 15. She started doing quads with 60-pound barbells. Now she's up to 300 pounds."

For her cardio work, Annika does mostly interval training: rope jumping and rollerblading, specifically. She changes routines every 8 weeks and works hardest in the off-season so that she can peak in the late winter/early spring for the first of four LPGA majors. The result of all this training is that Sörenstam has become leaner (14 percent body fat) and stronger. She drives 25 yards longer and hits straighter.

What can better physical fitness do for your golf game? It can take you farther than you ever thought possible, because it is through dedication to the fitness component that you will be able to work on the mechanical aspects of your swing. You will hit better shots and therefore improve your mental outlook as well. In short, a serious program of golf training can be 100 percent successful only if it includes a strong regimen of fitness, diet, and overall health. So let's get started!

Proper Goal Setting

By doing a close examination of the strengths and weaknesses uncovered in this phase, each golfer should be in a position to set some clear objectives moving forward with her game. This process will be different for each golfer and will be based on the commitment, dedication, and time allotted to improvement. As we enter the technical phase of training, golfers should have a written version of the specific goals they want to attain over the next 3 months, 6 months, and 1 year. For junior golfers, the process may be longer, requiring a 3- to 5-year plan.

Although goal setting may be an individual process, your list of goals should always include a specific desired outcome and a time frame to achieve the goals as well as clear-cut action steps that build one upon the other to get you to your destination in the shortest time. Goals should always be in a written format so that you can refer to them on a regular basis and make sure they are slightly to moderately out of reach. This ensures that they are realistic so that you—the student—will be motivated to work hard. Here are some more important reasons why goal setting is at the crux of an effective golf development program:

- Goal setting is the purpose of an action.

- Goals keep everyone on target.

- Goals commit you to the work, time, sacrifice, and whatever else is part of the price of achieving success.

- Goals provide you with a sense of purpose and direction as well as stimulating challenges.

- Goals maintain motivation.

- Goals direct attention.

- Goals increase effort.

- Goals help determine what is important to you.

- If you are having motivational problems, there is a high probability you also are experiencing performance problems.

- As long as you are succeeding and moving toward a meaningful goal, the chances are extremely high that you will maintain a consistent level of motivation.

Key Elements of the Assessment Phase: Technical, Mental, and Physical Summary

1. Take your golf fitness tests and record your score.
2. Clearly identify the weaknesses and limitations that are holding you back from a better round of golf.
3. Perform mental game self-evaluation.
4. Create an action plan that is based on your specific results.
5. Identify where you want your game to be in 3 months, 6 months, and 1 year.
6. Rate the elements of your game from 1 to 10.

Chapter 4
Technical Phase

By reading this book and applying what you learn, you're making a commitment to achieve your full potential as a golfer. In essence, you're creating a whole new way of looking at and doing things; you're building a whole new you by getting your body, mind, and swing mechanics to peak performance levels.

Just like everything else that has ever been created, from skyscrapers to works of art, this goal comes to fruition only after several stages: the conception of the idea, a plan for executing it, the assembling of the raw materials, and then the act of creation. So far in this book we've covered the idea and the plan. Now it's time to start building the new you, and as with any building process, the action begins by constructing a solid foundation that will support the rest of the process.

Building the Foundation to Realize Your Potential

It is during the technical phase of golf training that swing mechanics take center stage. Now that the assessments are complete, golfers can break their swings down through drills and practice techniques. This is an intensive period during which a golfer's once-familiar swing may feel completely foreign. It is also the phase in which a golfer's physical fitness plan is put into effect, giving the golfer's body the strength and flexibility to make the necessary swing changes.

From a mental perspective, golfers should be prepared to begin understanding how their thinking process affects their emotional states and behaviors on the course. A universal concept that every golfer can learn to embrace and apply immediately is the "one-shot-at-a-time model," which trains a player to stay in the present. If you can give every shot the planning, preparation, routine, and execution it requires without letting negative pictures or self-talk from a previous shot or experience influence your performance, you will be able to play at your highest level of ability.

In the technical stage, we're concerned with how your body feels when it swings the club and the specific motions of the body at different positions in the swing. We're more concerned about how the impact feels than about where the ball is going. The more we can reduce the sensory input for the player, the more likely it is that that golfer will be paying attention to the things that

make the golf swing effective and sustainable for long-term consistency.

Ideally, golfers will be hitting into a net and also taking practice swings in front of a mirror or using small sponge balls, paying little or no attention to ball flight. When a golfer isn't focused on what is happening to the ball, he or she is free to think: "Did I resist with my hips?" "Did my shoulders turn the way I wanted them to?" or "Did my body weight shift proportionately from my right to my left?" Once a player has gotten to a place where he or she is capable of executing these changes on the range reasonably and consistently, he or she is ready for the next stage. The golfer also will start to notice that his or her swing is more natural and the contact a lot more solid.

Technical Game Emphasis

The technical phase of training is among the most important for any level of play from recreational to professional. No golfer ever feels a sense of perfection with herself or with her game—just varying degrees of comfort and confidence.

Making sure that your fundamentals are solid can ensure long-term success. Many golfers make false assumptions about the fundamentals of grip, posture, and alignment because they think they mastered those specifics when they first learned to play golf. Thus, many golfers feel that the fundamentals apply only to beginners at the game.

Seasoned professionals understand that their technique can get sloppy or suffer through various parts of a season. Corrections and adjustments to keep themselves on track are all part of the process of development. You may recall that in 2006 Tiger Woods took 9 weeks off from golf after the death of his father.

After that significant layoff, he indicated in his first press conference that he was ready to compete in the 106th U.S. Open. "I'm very excited the way I've played at home, and even more excited the way I've played here," Woods, age 30, said at the Winged Foot Golf Club in Mamaroneck, New York.

According to the Associated Press, Woods initially found the thought of playing hard to bear because it would remind him of his father, Earl, who had taught him the game.

"I really had no desire to get back to the game of golf because of all the memories," Woods said. But when he finally took out his clubs, he found that the memories, in fact, made him happy.

"It was hard times going out there late in the evening like I always do," he said. "Any time you take time off and start back, you always work on your fundamentals: grip, posture, stance, alignment. Well, that's what I learned from Dad. It brought back so many great memories, and every time I thought back, I always had a smile on my face."

The technical phase of training is critical because it is the foundation of training. This cycle is used to identify weakness in the technical areas of the swing and the short game and to make corrections in technique. A golfer's level of progress and performance are dependent on his or her commitment and adaptation to training.

Hallmarks of the Technical Phase

- Use a mirror to watch yourself from various angles of your swing. Use slow-motion swings.

- Seek the help of a swing coach to videotape your swing and play it back repeatedly, making observations and notes on what needs to be improved.

- Take lessons during this period. Be sure to take at least one lesson on the short game and one lesson on the golf swing.

- Use swing training and teaching aids such as a medicine ball, a sponge ball, impact bags, and swing sticks, among other tools, to focus on swing positions.

- Make a thorough equipment evaluation, using a professional club fitter. Ensure that each club in your bag is properly fitted to your body and swing. If you are not sure of this, visit your local club or golf retailer for a proper fitting.

- Give equal time to the long game and the short game. The technical phase typically lasts 2 weeks in the off-season or pre-season, depending on the player's level of proficiency.

- Have a swing thought and feel the positions.

Where Not to Place Your Focus

- Do not be concerned with ball flight. Remember to focus on the proper "feel" and technique. Ball flight only serves as a mental distraction.

- This can be a frustrating period for golfers at all levels, and so patience is a necessity as you learn new skills.

- Try not to focus on results. They will come with time. Stay focused on the process of learning.

- If you play golf during this phase, do not keep score. During this phase you can hit several balls, staying focused on the changes.

During the swing analysis in this phase, the primary objective is to build confidence in the golf swing. Being a consistent player requires not only improvement in a golfer's technical proficiency but the confidence that comes with it. With the wide variety of golf swing instruction manuals on the market today, this book will not tackle the basics of grip, posture, and alignment or go over specific "how to perform the golf swing" instruction points. Instead, use the following drills to reinforce proper body motion and the positions of the golf swing.

Keep in mind that these drills should be done at a slow and deliberate pace. The goal of this process is to have a more clear understanding of your swing, develop the right feel for your body motion and movement patterns, and build confidence in your abilities as a player. In any part of your game—driving, putting, chipping, pitching, bunker play—a solid setup over the golf ball will allow you to swing more on plane and be a lot more consistent.

The setup helps the motion of the swing and allows a golfer to swing the club in balance. When you swing the club in balance, it's going to feel light throughout the swing. You're also going to keep the clubface square. Each element—grip, posture, and alignment—affects the others, and together they affect the ability to keep the clubface square, which improves the path of the club, the direction of the ball, and body position at impact. Once these elements are improved, you'll have a body that moves in sync with your club, and that will allow you to be more aggressive through the ball, creating more power, better control, and good direction.

Training in a Technical Week

All golf swing drills in the technical phase will focus on the following:

1. Preparation: grip, posture, alignment
2. Setup
3. Body motion
4. The six steps of the golf swing
5. Club awareness drills
6. Motion drills

Preparation: Grip, Posture, and Alignment

The Grip

Purpose: The grip is essential to controlling the clubface throughout the swing. The purpose of a good grip is to keep the face of the club square throughout the swing; that will allow you to control your direction and trajectory. Controlling your swing will build confidence in your game.

Grip Drills

Grip Position A

1. Start by making sure that the clubface is square so that the leading edge is straight up and down.

2. Place the club in your left hand, making sure the palm of that hand is facing down. The club should run diagonally from the palm to the index finger.

Grip Position B

1. Close the left hand, making sure that two knuckles are visible.

2. The left thumb should be on top of the shaft, slightly to the right of center.

Grip Position C

1. The "V" formation between the thumb and the forefinger should point between your right ear and shoulder.

2. The left-hand grip is held in the palm and the fingers.

Grip Position D

1. The right-hand grip is predominantly in the fingers, and the club runs along the base of the fingers at a slight diagonal.

2. Wrap your right hand around the club and fit the left thumb into the center of the right palm.

There are three types of grips:

**Interlock Grip
(Advanced Players)**

**Overlap Grip
(Advanced Players)**

**Ten-Finger Grip (Beginners
and Intermediate Players)**

Left-Hand-Grip Drills

Purpose: To feel the grip in the fingers of your left hand and make
sure the back of your left hand matches the clubface.

a. Place the club diagonally in front of you, across your body.

b. Grip the club in your fingers, making sure the back of
your left hand matches the clubface.

a. Place the club in your left hand with the left arm by your side.

b. Make sure the clubface is square and feel the left thumb
slightly right of center.

Bring the club in front of your body and place the right
hand correctly on the club.

Now your grip will be correct, and you should have a sense
of feel in both hands. Your grip should feel firm, and your
arms and shoulders should be comfortable and relaxed.

Posture

The swing is an athletic movement. Good posture allows you to swing the club on plane and maximize your speed and power. An athletic posture is the foundation for the swing, allowing your upper body and lower body to work together.

Posture Drill

Side View   Front View

Position A

1. Make sure your feet are shoulder width apart (the shorter the club, the narrower the stance).

2. Point your toes slightly outward— approximately 30 degrees—to help transfer weight.

3. Stand straight and hold the club vertically in front of your body.

Position B

1. Bend your knees slightly, keeping your arms straight in front of your body

2. Feel the weight move toward the balls of your feet, bending from the hip joints—not the waist.

Position C

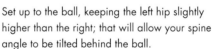

Set up to the ball, keeping the left hip slightly higher than the right; that will allow your spine angle to be tilted behind the ball.

Position D

Good posture is the foundation of an athletic swing.

Alignment

Alignment is the way you line your body up toward the target. Set the clubface square to the target and align your body around it. When you are setting up for a straight shot, your body should be aligned parallel to the target line. This includes feet, knees, hips, eyes, and shoulders. Ball position controls alignment, so make sure your ball is placed correctly.

Alignment Drill

When setting up, make sure to aim first with the face of the club. Then align your body square to the face. Use this drill to get a good feel for your alignment. You can remove the middle club and practice the shot.

Right-Side View

Left-Side View

Front View

1. One way to practice good alignment is to lay three clubs on the ground.

2. Place the first club on the line of the target that sits directly behind the clubface to keep the clubface square.

3. The second club should be placed directly between the ball and your toes so that you can align your feet, shoulders, and hips correctly.

4. The third club sits outside the ball to help you maintain your swing path.

Grip, posture, and alignment are the key elements of a good setup. Practice the drills regularly and make sure to keep a consistent routine with your setup practice. Setting up with different clubs will affect ball position and the width of your stance.

8 Iron

With a short iron, the ball position is off the left eye and the stance is narrower.

5 Iron

With a 5 iron, the ball position is farther forward off the left ear. The stance is wider.

Driver

When you set up with the driver, the ball will be between the left shoulder and the left ear, and the stance is widest.

Body Motion

Body motion is the winding and unwinding of the upper body back and through the golf swing. The lower body resists the turning of the upper body in the backswing, and that resistance unleashes power at impact. The coiling of the body around the spine angle controls the weight shift from one side of the body to the other, allow-ing the arms to swing through impact. Pivots are excellent drills to practice because they help you improve your stability, flexibility, and tempo. The pivot is the essence of the golf swing—moving around your spine—and by working on controlling the movement of your body, you will have more control of your arms and a better feel for impact.

Club Across the Shoulders Drills

a. Place the club in front of your shoulders, cross your arms, and assume the setup position.

b. Make sure the left shoulder is slightly higher than the right.

a. Feel your left shoulder move down and across over your right knee.

b. Your head will move slightly to the right, and your weight will shift to the right side.

c. In the transition, feel your left knee, left hip, and left shoulder move away from your right side and shift the weight to your left side.

Uncoil the upper body and feel your right shoulder move across over your left knee.

Finish the drill with your weight on the left side and your right shoulder facing the target.

There are many different pivot drills that you can use during training and practice.

Here are a few more drill ideas that you can incorporate into your practice program:

Club Behind Shoulders

Split-Handed

Crossover Hands

Club over Right Arm

The Six Steps of the Golf Swing

Golfers in search of a more consistent golf swing need to learn how to swing the club in balance. The six steps of the golf swing were developed to help guide and direct golfers at all levels into the specific positions throughout all phases of the swing. Among those first critical steps is the "moveaway," which gives golfers a feel for the first move of the club away from the ball. This sets into motion the sequence of events that allows you to set the backswing in motion and place the club in the proper position at the top of your swing.

Golf Swing Steps

Side View

Step 1: Moveaway Position

Front View

Step 2: Halfway Back Position

Side View

Front View

Step 3: Top of the Backswing

Step 4: Transition

Step 5: Impact

Step 6: Finish

Club Awareness Drills

Plane Drill

Purpose: To feel the club in balance and create the right positions during the swing.

How to perform the drill: Grip down on the club so that you can see the grip end between your arms. Make sure the club is off the ground.

Moveaway Drill

Purpose: To help you feel your moveaway. This drill will give you a feel of the clubface being square throughout your swing. You also will feel your grip more in the fingers.

How to perform the drill: Take your athletic setup. Grip way down on the club: about 8 inches from the clubhead. Then place the grip end on your left hip.

Two-Club Balance Drill

Purpose: This will help you build strength and a solid swing plane. It forces you to swing both clubs in balance using your arms, wrists, and upper body while keeping the lower body stable.

How to perform the drill: Grip two clubs—one in each hand—and make sure to choke up on the clubs, starting with both of them off the ground. Keep your hands a few inches apart during the drill.

Motion Drills

Finger Down the Shaft

Purpose: This drill helps keep the clubface square throughout the swing and improves the impact position. It is perfect for beginning, intermediate, and advanced players.

How to perform the drill: Assume your setup position. Extend your right index finger down the shaft, making sure that the right-hand "V" is pointing to your right ear. Make a three-quarter golf swing and release your right hand at impact, which will cause the ball to draw.

Split-Handed Drill

Purpose: This will help you with your move-away off the ball. It also will help you set the club in the backswing and teach you how to release the club through impact. It is designed for beginning, intermediate, and advanced players.

How to perform the drill: Place your hands in normal grip position. Move your right hand slightly down the shaft; leave hands a few inches apart. Your right thumb will be near the end of the grip. Practice your moveaway as you take the club into a full backswing and back through impact.

Squatty 3-Wood Drill for All Levels

Purpose: The squatty 3 wood will help develop stability and power in your swing.

How to perform the drill: Widen your stance at setup. Lower your hands and squat as though you are sitting down. Position the ball slightly back in your stance and make a half swing back and through, keeping the lower body still.

Right Foot Back Drill

Purpose: This drill, for beginning, intermediate, and advanced players, will increase resistance in the backswing and give you the feeling of hitting into a firm left side.

How to perform the drill: Take your normal stance and move your right foot back, with your right toe in line with the left heel. Make a three-quarter backswing, keeping the upper body centered. Swing into a firm left side.

Purpose: This drill will prevent you from swaying off the ball in the backswing and help your body coil into a firm right side.

How to perform the drill: Take your normal stance and place your left foot back, with the toe in line with the right heel. Make a three-quarter backswing, feeling the resistance in the right leg as you uncoil through the downswing.

Purpose: This drill helps keep the plane of your swing in front of your body throughout the swing. When you stand with your heels on the board, your weight is on the balls of your feet, preventing you from swinging too much on the inside in the downswing.

How to Perform the Drill: Place your heels on the board. Feel your weight more toward your toes. Make a full swing, keeping your balance throughout. (You also can perform this drill with your toes on the board to give you a feel of shallowing the club in the downswing. Or try placing your feet on the board to keep your weight balanced and maintain stability in your lower body.)

Mental Game Emphasis

There are several schools of thought about what helps players get better at the game of golf. There are some who believe that spending many hours hitting shots and rolling putts is the key. There are others who believe that just playing the game—being out on the golf course as much as possible—is the way to achieve competence. Still others think that having an instructor stand at a player's side while he or she hits balls, rolls putts, or plays the game is the way to get it done.

What's the "right" answer? A little bit of all of these. Although one can always point to individual exceptions to almost any rule, the truth is that there is a common thread among most successful golfers. That thread ensures that there is a developmental plan that incorporates all the elements of the game and that the golfer has a purpose in mind each time he or she has a golf club in hand—in the practice areas as well as on the course.

It is not enough to have raw physical talent. The courses throughout the country and beyond are full of players who did not achieve what many thought their physical potential was. It is not enough simply to hit balls repeatedly on the range without some sense of what one is trying to accomplish and some feedback about whether that's being accomplished. It is not enough simply to make a tee time, play 18 holes, and hope some lessons are learned along the way.

Sport science research shows that the task of becoming an expert at a game such as golf requires that a golfer identify and learn skills that

will create more consistency. Developing those skills includes having the player monitor and control his performance, become more aware of his limitations and strengths, and recognize how to make adjustments in specific conditions. In other words, it is critical that there be a constant "feedback loop" on what is working and what is not and specific strategies to address the things that are not working very well.

Make sure that the time spent on the golf course, practice range, or putting green is productive. Identify an area for improvement, have a plan for how to enhance that area, and pay attention to these things when you're playing. That's the way to learn the fastest and learn the most about how to be the player you want to be!

There are some important concepts for players to understand about how their thinking process affects their emotional states and behavior.

Golfers need a basis for understanding activation and arousal levels and how maintaining a sense of calm from a psychological and mental perspective helps enhance their performance. It's important for them to recognize that their self-dialog and self-concepts ultimately affect the way they play the game. These are among the most critical concepts taught to players in the technical phase of development.

The Game within the Game: Priming Your Mind for Success

Even though golfers at all levels realize that perhaps as much as half the challenge in golf is mental, very few attempt to train their minds for competition. There's an old adage that golf is 90 percent mental. Whether or not that is the case depends on the player, but even if that's the way you feel, we're not suggesting that you spend 90 percent of your time training your brain. What we are suggesting is that you challenge yourself to devote more time to that training than you currently do. You can begin to do this by using the following points to help you understand the benefits of improving this vital aspect of your game.

Competitive golf is played mainly on a five-and-a-half-inch course: the space between your ears.

—*Bobby Jones*

Everything Begins with Thought

Almost everything you do in the mental aspect of your game comes down to three things: thinking, feeling, and behavior. That's the order in which things occur, but it's easier to understand them if you consider them in reverse. What you do (behavior) is influenced by your emotions (feeling), which are created by your thoughts (thinking).

Here's an example to illustrate how this works: Imagine that you're standing over a 4-foot putt. The putt breaks a little right to left, and you're committed to starting the ball on a line toward the right edge of the hole. The putt is a little uphill, and so you know you can hit the putt with reasonable firmness. Now let's pause in the process for a moment.

If you're thinking about these factors in advance of striking the ball, you probably also will have feelings of confidence. These feelings (perhaps preceded by the thought "I'm capable of rolling this ball on that line") most likely will engender the behavior of you executing a reasonably smooth stroke. As long as your technique is sound, you stand an excellent chance of getting the ball in the hole.

Now let's go back to where you paused earlier and continue imagining. While you're standing over the ball, you acknowledge to yourself that this 4-foot putt is not only for a birdie, it also will result in the lowest score you've ever shot for one round. In addition, your brain reminds you that you've missed two putts of the same length in the last few holes.

Do these thoughts change things? The answer depends completely on which thoughts rise to the forefront. If you are *thinking* about the potential meaning of the putt ("I could break 80 for the first time!") or about your past efforts ("Don't blow another opportunity here!"), you are opening the door to countless *emotions*, including excitement, doubt, worry, and fear. These emotions have the potential to influence your *behavior* in ways that affect your tempo, rhythm, tension level, and stroke.

Consider these scenarios, and it is clear that you are much more likely to get the ball in the hole in the first than you are in the second. The valuable thing to realize in these two scenarios is that you didn't change what you were asking of yourself: a 4-foot putt is a 4-foot putt regardless of how you choose to think about it. When a player says, "That putt scared the heck out of me," one can only wonder, "How so?" What did it do to the player? The ball was just sitting there motionless!

To be clear, then, a change in your thinking has the potential to affect what you're paying attention to, *which in turn* can affect your behavior to the point where you associate the circumstance (4-foot putt for birdie) with a negative outcome ("I struggle with those").

More accurately, most players do not "struggle" with 4-foot putts. They instead struggle in their *thinking* about 4-foot putts. Have you ever thought to yourself, "I can make these all day on the practice green, so how come I can't make them out here on the course?"

The answer, in part, is that the type and quality of your thoughts change out on the course. The other part of the answer is that you've labeled yourself as someone who struggles with particular things on the course.

Taking Charge of Your Thoughts

To play superb golf you must be in control of, as Bobby Jones put it, "the space between your ears." The first step toward doing that is to be aware of and take responsibility for your thoughts. Changing your thinking on the course (and even in everyday life) is a very simple process: All you have to do is pay attention to the types of thoughts you have and change them into more helpful thoughts. The process for recognizing your thoughts and improving them consists of the following:

• Identify incorrect/unhealthy thinking.

• Stop the stream of thoughts/pictures.

• Change to more correct/healthy thinking.

Seems simple enough, yes? Yet many people struggle with this process because poor thinking habits are ingrained over the years, and even if these people commit to trying, they spend too little time practicing their new way of thinking.

The good news is that you don't have to struggle with this idea because the process is completely within your control. You have the power to choose the thoughts in your mind, and given how many things in this game are outside of your control, you should derive confidence from knowing there is *something* you can influence!

The Four P's

Once you've identified some of the thoughts and pictures that are unhealthy for your game, the question to ask yourself is: What should I be thinking? What would be more helpful? When the greatest golf minds in the world are engaged out on the course, they focus on the four P's:

• **P**resent

• **P**rocess

• **P**ositive

• **P**atient

Once again, it sounds simple enough, so let's take a look at how your mind should process the four P's.

Present

In everything you do in life, there's the ever-present danger of spending too much time looking to the past or future while ignoring what's going on right now. For certain, occasional glimpses into the rearview mirror can provide you with information that is helpful, just as a quick flash to the future allows you to plan ahead in the chess match you play against each hole. The key, however, is to limit those moments to glimpses that provide information and *not* allow them to become obsessions (or stares, if you will).

You'll know a glimpse has turned into a stare when you have thoughts such as these:

> "I should have done it differently."
> "I can't believe I screwed that up; it was so easy."

These are examples of backward looking and thinking that can inhibit your ability to play to your potential *right now*. It is nearly impossible to perform at a peak level when you are focusing on something other than what you're about to do. Most of us are not talented enough (or lucky enough) to think about the past and still react to the situation at hand in an optimal way.

Similarly, getting caught up in the future can deflect you from focusing on *this moment*. Clues that you're spending too much time on the future are characterized by "what if" and "I hope I don't" thoughts such as the following:

> "I hope I don't hook it into the water."
> "I hope I don't run this downhill putt too far past the hole."
> "What if my swing breaks down when the match is on the line?"

A tour player may have similar thoughts:

> "What if my swing breaks down during the last round?"
> "What if I miss the cut?"

Here's the really tricky part. Sometimes we future-think about positive things:

> "If I just par the next three holes, I'll break 90 for the first time."
> "If I win one of the next three holes, I'll win the club championship."

Thoughts like that can't be bad, right? The power of positive thinking is well documented, right? Not exactly. Even if these thoughts *feel* positive, they are, in fact, a distraction from being focused on the present.

To *be present* means to purposefully anchor yourself in the now so that you put all your mental energy into executing *this task, this moment*! When you are on the course and the types of distracting thoughts described above come to mind, refocus by gently bringing your thinking back to the present or by restarting your pre-shot routine.

You can learn from the past when the round is over so that you know what to focus on during practice time on the range, and you should glimpse the future for strategic reasons during a round. But when it's time to play the shots, there's only one place for your thoughts to be: *right here, right now.*

Process

Even after you've secured your mind in the present, you still have to direct it toward the "process" or task at hand. Most players think in terms of results, outcomes, or consequences (e.g., thinking about making a birdie putt instead of focusing on the execution of the stroke required). While you're in action on the course, thoughts of winning and succeeding actually can inhibit your performance:

"If I make this birdie, I go to two under par."

This type of thinking is typical at all levels, and sometimes, despite poor thinking, the putt is holed. However, if you recognize this type of thinking while it's happening and put yourself back in the process ("Focus on rolling this putt toward the right edge"), you will discover that you can execute more consistently in competition over time.

Staying in the process is extremely challenging for players at every level because the tendency to think and speak in terms of results is part of the paradigm of the game. You, for example, may say to yourself before a match, "If I win this match, I move on to the semifinals of the club championship." And after the match, everyone you see will ask, "How'd you do?" or "Did you win?"

Even for tour players, pre-round discussions are rife with consequence and outcome questions such as "What do you think you'll have to shoot to make the cut?" and "What was the number that won last year's event?" And after the round, other players or the media ask: "What did you shoot?" "Where did you finish?" "How many birdies did you make?"

The emphasis that is placed on outcome by other people is very difficult to overcome. However, if you listen to the top players talk after a round, they routinely say they stayed in the process of hitting each shot as well as possible and didn't worry about other people, how other players were playing, or what number they'd have to shoot.

Positive

There is a psychological theory that stipulates that all of our behavior falls into two basic categories. We either behave to get something we want or act to avoid something we don't want. Sigmund Freud called this the pleasure/pain principle. We seek pleasure and stay away from pain whether or not we're conscious of that motivation.

Whether or not you put much stock in Freud, this theory has very real applications to you as a player. The players who think the most effectively are those who have a mental picture of the type of shot they desire.

> "I want to hit a draw, starting on a line toward that tree just beyond the fairway."
> "I'm going to roll this downhill putt so that it dies right in the hole."
> "I'm going to slow my tempo down so that I can put a smooth swing on the ball."

Those who struggle with this thought process more commonly fill their heads with pictures or words that describe things they're trying to avoid.

> "Don't hit it left here."
> "Don't blow this by the hole or you might be looking at a 3-footer coming back."
> "Don't start the club so far inside."
> "Stop swinging so darned fast."

Although avoidance motivation can be very powerful, its weakness is that it's influenced primarily by fear. No matter how talented or skilled you are, it's very difficult to play your best consistently when you're consumed by fear. The challenge for all of us in golf is to keep our thoughts and the pictures in our minds on the things that we *desire*. This motivation is healthier for the psyche, easier on the blood pressure, and more likely to produce the results over time that we're working toward.

Patient

Few—if any—sports require the level of patience that golf does. Whether they are big-picture things such as the development of your swing or short-term moments such as rebounding after a double bogey, patience is a key element in the mind-sets of the best players. Impatience can lead to a number of maladies, including unrealistic expectations, ill-advised course management strategies, increased tension and tempo, lack of commitment to a shot, incomplete gathering of pre-shot information, and distraction from the task. All these things—and countless others—lead to less fun, higher numbers, and less satisfaction with your scores.

In contrast, patient players realize that in the pursuit of excellence, progress is generally very slow and is measured in very small increments.

Additionally, patient players look for opportunities during a round to take calculated risks within the context of an overall game plan. They are not influenced to swing hard (and abandon tempo and rhythm) or to cut short pre-shot preparation, nor do they make poor shot-selection decisions because they're annoyed, are irritated by the previous shot, or feel rushed or frustrated by their surroundings.

No matter what the situation is, patient players take in objective information, make fully informed decisions, and commit to their choice. That's patience in action, and that's how the best players train themselves to think.

Golf Fitness Emphasis

All golfers want more power in their swing and more distance off the tee. The majority of today's golfers would agree that achieving this begins with fitness. However, there is a specific process within the achievement of fitness for developing this kind of raw power, and it begins with the assessment phase.

True power is a natural expression in any sport when a person's body parts have a sufficient amount of strength and are free to move through a full range of motion. Watch the power of a baseball player as he hits a home run or a pitcher as he winds up for a strike across the mound. There is beauty in motion!

A large part of developing this kind of power is finding the areas that are creating restrictions and thus allowing shortened movement patterns and golf swing inconsistencies. At first glance, many consider themselves flexible because they can touch their toes or reach for the sky with tall arms and freely moving shoulders. Yet a golfer may not know to look for a restricted right hip or tight right spine yielding difficulties in her backswing and taking the clubhead off its intended path. Any interruption of movement is a swing fault and a source of frustration for a golfer at any level.

The assessment phase uncovers the areas that are weak and need more strength. It also uncovers areas that are tight or restricted. This technical phase is thus all about learning good movement patterns that lead to better motion in your swing. The physical side of golf is designed to complement—not compete with—the technical and mental elements. Yes, patience is required, as is a desire to learn the basics of movement so that golfers can build upon this sequence and increase their exercise intensity and volume in later stages. There are certain movement patterns that serve as the basis or foundation for all fitness exercises performed as your body progresses. Each is designed to be a teaching tool for golf movement patterns and the development of strength, stability, flexibility, and mobility. Each creates a more balanced approach to your body as it corrects deficiencies in your body and your swing. By now you should see how they are related. The goal of the technical phase is to develop good workout habits, improve body motion, increase conditioning, and create greater freedom of movement.

I've worked extremely hard to strengthen the stabilizer muscles in my hips and legs as well as improve my core body strength. . . . My driving has been the chief benefactor of all that work.

—*Phil Mickelson*

Principles of Golf Athletic Development

Here are the important training concepts to embrace as you begin your fitness training in the technical phase of development:

- **Vary your planes of motion**. Golf fitness training always includes exercises that have varying planes of motion. These movement patterns include front-to-back motions, left-to-right motions, and rotational exercises. That variety allows you to explore your freedom of movement and prepare your body for the demands of golf.

- **Keep movements ground-based**. There has been a recent craze with the use of fitness balls, foam rollers, and other balance aids. It is always fun to learn new movements and try different exercises, but never forget that golf is played while standing on one's feet and by transferring force from the ground up. Don't be afraid to mix in some of your favorite exercises while lying or sitting on the floor or across a fitness ball but keep them to a minimum. Ground-based movements that focus on natural force production are your best bet for golf.

- **Build a foundation, first and foremost**. Learning how to engage the core muscles properly provides a platform of stability and a level of protection from injury. To keep your body from breaking down and affecting your golf swing negatively, exercises aimed at restoring muscular balance should be a natural part of program design. As you continue to build foundational strength, you also improve your resistance to fatigue. Focus on the foundation first, and all the other desirable golf qualities will follow.

- **Integrate multiple elements into each exercise**. Each weekly workout should address all the important elements of golf, including flexibility, core development, balance, mobility, general athletic movement, strength, and power. Integrated training techniques will develop your skills in each of these areas and produce a whole new level of play. Examples of integration include a 5-minute dynamic warm-up and a roughly 30-minute strength routine, followed by 10 to 15 minutes of stretches. Each workout can be broken down into strength development for several weeks, core stabilization for several weeks, and power development as you move into peak season.

- **Progressive resistance**. Strength should be developed in a progressive manner. To get stronger, one needs to add resistance progressively over time relative to previous workouts. Strength gains are made slowly but consistently, and you will see the difference in your game in no time. Without progress in your program, you're limiting your potential. Progression also involves varying your speeds of movement as your body becomes more adapted to each exercise.

- **Train movements, not individual muscles**. Sport-specific training is different from general fitness training and vastly different from old-school body-building. For decades we have learned where our large muscle groups and small muscle groups are located. We have been taught that to develop each muscle, we must contract it to help it grow in size and strength. One of the most talked about isolation exercises is the biceps curl. "Isolation" of muscle structure has been replaced with a more dynamic approach to sport-specific training called "integration." Through time, research, and new techniques, athletes and trainers have learned that sports conditioning requires the synchronization of many body parts in order to perform a sport-specific movement. We have learned that in order to be your best, you must train according to the demands of your sport as well as your position and individual talents. In golf, many muscle groups work in a coordinated fashion to produce explosive strength and power, and they should be trained as such.

- **Train explosively**. The amount of force needed for any activity is supplied by the use of two different types of motor units in the body: fast twitch and slow twitch. Each type varies greatly in its ability to generate force. Fast-twitch fibers are much better at generating short bursts of strength or speed, but they succumb to fatigue more readily. Golfers, like sprinters, basketball players, and other quick-burst athletes, count on fast-twitch muscle fibers to fire more rapidly, which creates more power. In contrast, slow-twitch fibers that are important in sports with long duration—marathon running and biking, for instance—fire more slowly but can last a long time before hitting fatigue.

- **Principle of variety**. Yes, the body has an amazing ability to adapt to imposed demands. Not only is variety the spice of life, it keeps the body guessing and, more important, progressing! There are many ways to add variety to any routine. This may include new exercises, changing the order of exercises, and changing the frequency or length of workouts. Loads can be increased and decreased depending on the repetition range and intensity of your stage in the fitness program. During the pre-comp phase, we overload the body so that it is always progressing at a moderate pace. In competitive stages the volume may decrease, but exercise selection changes still can create variety along with the training responses you desire.

- **Periodize your program into split routines**. In the golden days of bodybuilding, split routines meant building the back and biceps one day and the triceps the next. Today these programs are considered archaic for most sports, and the same is true in golf. The most efficient routine for athletes to use is referred to as a split routine. This routine consists of alternating the types of exercises performed and executing them on alternate days—for example, performing explosive lifts on Monday and Thursday and strength lifts on Tuesday and Friday. The split routine allows an individual's body to recover from one set of activities while it engages in others.

- **General strength, then golf-specific**. You will notice a deliberate move from an emphasis on building general strength in the technical phase to more directed or "golf-specific" exercises as we transition into the pre-comp phase. This is by design, as all golfers can benefit from building the foundational elements of power before tapping into their full potential in the later stages of development. As a golfer learns the basics of transferring force and loads throughout his or her body and as the season gets closer, more guided and golf-specific movements are desired. Many trainers, coaches, and players may refer to this as training for "specificity," where training more closely mimics the demands of the sport.

- **Injury prevention.** A large part of training is keeping an athlete injury-free. Depending on his or her history of exercise and past injuries, this can be a daunting task. To prevent common injuries in golf, it is important to understand how and when they occur. Some golfers find continued weakness in the shoulder girdle, whereas others can't seem to get rid of tightness or pain in the low back. Nobody is immune to injuries in golf or in any sport in which the task is repetitive and is carried out over an extended period. However, proper training can ensure a stronger, healthier athletic body that usually is able to withstand or ward off common injuries.

- **Nutrition and recovery.** Proper nutrition and rest help meet the energy demands of training. The body requires six separate types of nutrients to function properly: carbohydrates, fats, proteins, vitamins, minerals, and water. It is important to consume a balance of different types of food to supply the necessary nutrients. An imbalance of these nutrients may cause undesirable adaptations, such as illness, injury, or excess body fat. Hardworking athletes go through a tremendous amount of stress as a result of their daily training cycles. Good nutrition strategies also can be used throughout the competitive phase as an advantage for the most serious golfers. Supplying your body with a constant slow-release food supply can ensure strong and consistent mental focus.

- **Core stability and postural control.** More efficient movement creates a more efficient swing. Golfers maintain an athletic posture over long periods and require both trunk and core stabilization and

endurance. By increasing your strength and endurance in the core region of your body, you provide a solid base of support for rotation in addition to the proper transfer of power throughout the body.

Most golfers understand the importance of good golf posture. Many professional golf instructors commonly refer to this as "spine angle." Although most golfers know this angle is critical to keep the club on plane, it is also important to eliminate injuries and improve their swinging action. What most golfers seek is a stable and strong golf posture so that they can create a powerful and effective golf swing without additional stress and strain. Body structure and posture are unique traits, but an improper golf swing can cause specific muscle imbalances. These imbalances may not be obvious until they cause a disruptive physical problem.

The body slowly adapts to poor posture, and some body parts, such as the neck, shoulder, back, and hip, may be overused to balance for loss of motion in other areas of the body. The goal of exercises for posture is to improve and then reinforce good, solid body positions as well as static and dynamic balance during the swing. The postural muscles are located throughout the body and serve to hold the skeletal system and joint structures in proper alignment.

Some common problems affected by posture are:

- Difficulty keeping your eye on the ball during your swing
- Difficulty transferring force from the lower body to the upper body
- Compromised swing patterns
- Poor clubhead speed and poor club control

Rules of Exercise Progression

The fundamental rules of progression for training the core are the same as those for training any other segment in the kinetic chain. Remember this favorite song from your childhood: The foot bone's connected to the leg bone. The leg bone's connected to the knee bone. The knee bone's connected to the thigh bone . . .

This was a simple song that helped us understand how the body is connected one segment at a time, forming a kinetic chain from the bottom to the top. Ironically, this is also how we learn to transfer force in the golf swing: from the bottom to the top.

To learn how to transfer the loads that the body is subjected to in the golf swing, there is a continuum in exercise progressions that can be an important part of your development process.

Progress from simple to complex: Begin your exercise program by mastering the simplest forms of exercises first. As these exercises become more comfortable, your body can be challenged further with more creative and demanding exercises. A golfer should learn proper stabilization techniques before increasing the demands on his or her body. An example of progression for the legs may be to perform two-leg ball squats before performing the one-leg version.

Progress from known to unknown: The exercise sequence should begin with controlled, low-neuromuscular-demand exercises. The golfer then should progress to less controlled, challenging exercises. Think about performing a set of abdominal crunches on the floor and then proceeding to a fitness ball.

Progress from low force to high force: Train with low-force, controlled movements until they can be mastered, and then proceed to higher-force, ballistic movements.

Progress from static to dynamic: Start with exercises in a stationary posture and then add more dynamic movements as those movements are mastered.

Training the Core

The "core" has to be one of the most overused buzzwords in golf fitness training. However, few golfers understand which muscles constitute the core, which exercises activate the core, and what an activated core feels like. This notion is one of the most fundamental in golf training yet probably is the most misunderstood.

The golf swing relies on proper core engagement and sufficient strength so that golfers can have good stability and control in their swing. Core conditioning is crucial for all golfers because all their movements stem from the strength in this area. Wherever you find a weak core, you find a major source of energy leaks in the golf swing.

The core is where the body's center of gravity is situated and where force production is generated. Since many golfers have a weak core, they also experience chronic posture problems. Over time, this creates wear and tear on the body. A golfer with a weak core is vulnerable to injury and struggles with swing efficiency. The muscles of the core include the abdominals and the muscles that surround the hips, the lumbar spine (low back), the thoracic spine (midback), and the cervical spine (upper back and neck).

In the beginning stages of fitness, it is important to learn how to activate the core. Let's start by explaining the proper feel of these muscles through different body positions.

Core Exercise 1: Stomach Pull

a. Notice that one arm is tucked underneath the lower back and one hand is touching the midstomach muscles.

b. Begin this exercise by pulling in your stomach muscles so that your low back feels flat against your lower hand.

c. Perform this exercise several times while focusing on the motion and "feel" of flattening your low back against your hand and toward the floor. This reinforces the feeling of a neutral posture position.

a. When you're ready, lift your knees to a 45-degree position and see if you can keep the same neutral position with your posture.

b. Many golfers will feel a loss of tension in the abdominal muscles. This is a sign that you need additional strengthening and reinforcing exercises for the midsection and postural muscles.

If you completed stage 2 without any problem, progress to alternating leg lifts between your left and your right while still concentrating on the same neutral posture position.

While doing position 3 in Core Exercise 1, did you shift from a "soft belly" to a "hard belly" feeling in your stomach muscles, or were you able to hold the same relative tension throughout your midsection? This is a strong indication of your ability to hold a solid spine angle throughout your golf swing when it is needed. Here, Steve Brown, an 8 handicap, is remembering this "feel" in his postural muscles just before beginning his setup position.

Core Exercise 2: The Plank

One of the key components of the plank exercise is a golfer's ability to maintain this position without any postural changes whatsoever. Far too many college golfers boast of their ability to maintain this position for 2 minutes or more. Yet when they perform this in person, it is obvious that significant body changes such as elevated gluteus muscles and significant swayback in the lower back muscles or a shifting of weight from one side of the body to the other is occurring. The golfer may be able to hold this position for an extended period, but these body position changes are a sure signal that more core work is needed.

Exercises in the future may not be core-specific, but they will always utilize core strength and control to orchestrate the movement. In other words, this "trained" body position of neutral posture is maintained through all future exercises. Although many trainers and golfers still advocate a specific core workout that is separate from the main workout, it is far more effective and efficient to learn a variety of complex, compound exercises that call on the core to complete the movement. Exercise variations and recommendations will be discussed further in the next chapter.

Here is a very popular exercise for core development among golfers. It most commonly is called "the plank," although it is recognized by other names as well. Golfers typically are instructed to hold this position as a way to measure core strength and endurance.

Super Eight for Strength

For golfers who found in the assessments section that they needed more strength in the upper body, the lower body, or both, here are simple, effective, and critical "Super 8" exercises every golfer should perform in the technical phase of physical development.

Golf Strength Drills

Golf Strength 1: Push-Up to Arm Lift

a. Begin in a push-up position with your arms placed shoulder width apart on a bench or chair.

b. Create tension in your core by squeezing in your stomach muscles so that your body forms one line from the head to the heels.

c. Push your body up slowly with both hands.

Upon the initial lift, pick up your right arm and extend it straight out. You immediately will notice activation of your core muscles while challenging your balance and upper-body strength.

Golf Strength 2: Cross-Body Elevated Plank

a. Place your left elbow on a bench with your legs extended out. Use only your body weight or place a light dumbbell in your right hand.

b. Your right arm will be in front of your body with the palms facing in.

Extend your arm up and away from your body.

Golf Strength 3: Med Ball Single-Leg Squat

① a. Place a medicine ball in your hands and stand in an athletic position.

b. Begin by raising one foot off the ground several inches, keeping your weight only slightly forward.

② a. Lower your body back and down as low as you can.

b. Push through your heel to return to the start position. If you do not have access to a medicine ball, just clasp your hands together to complete the exercise.

Golf Strength 4: Lateral Walks

① a. Place a miniband around your ankles.

b. Assume an athletic posture with the knees slightly bent and the shoulders back and down.

② a. Take one step to the side to create tension in your lower body, specifically the glutes and hips.

b. Continue stepping to one side until you have reached 12 repetitions.

c. Then begin taking steps as you lead with the opposite leg, again for 12 repetitions.

Golf Strength 5: Cook Lift

This exercise was popularized by the physical therapist Gray Cook website: (http://www.functionalmovement.com).

a. Begin by lying on your back with both knees bent.

b. Place your hands around one knee and bring it toward your chest.

a. Push off your remaining foot and lift your glutes as high as possible.

b. Slowly lower to the start position.

Golf Strength 6: Forward and Back Lunge

a. Place both hands around a medicine ball with the body in an athletic position.

b. Take one large step backward into a lunge. Extend both arms straight out as you lunge backward.

a. Place your weight on your back foot and then return to the start position.

b. Now take a large step forward. Use the weight on your front foot to push yourself back to the start position.

Golf Strength 7: Medicine Ball Back and Through

a. Sit on an abdominal crunch bench with your feet in a secure position.

b. Place both hands around a medicine ball. Make sure you do not round (flex) your back in this position.

Rotate your body to your backswing position and then to your follow-through position.

Golf Strength 8: Plank to a Back Row

Begin by placing your body into a plank position with both hands on the floor or with each hand holding a dumbbell. Your body should extend in a straight line from the head to the heels.

a. Pick up one dumbbell on either side of your body and begin a back row movement by bringing your bent elbow up and toward the ceiling. Try to keep your body position the same, as golfers with a weak core will compensate by shifting their body weight to one side or the other.

b. Place the hand or dumbbell back on the ground and pull the opposite arm into a back row.

Super Six for Flexibility

There is no question that the need for increased mobility and flexibility is among the top concerns for golfers of all ages and abilities. The chief threats to a golfer's game include tightness or movement restrictions of the spine, shoulders, and hips. These three areas account for almost every major swing fault a golfer encounters. Take a look at how you performed on the flexibility tests in the assessment phase. Which stretches do you need to do more often?

Flexibility Drills

Flexibility 1: Hip Stretch

a. Bend the front and back legs to 90 degrees.

b. Place one hand inside the thigh and the other hand outside the same thigh.

Keep a flat back and bend forward from the hip as far as you can, maintaining the same spine angle.

Flexibility 2: Kneeling Midback Stretch

a. Kneel on the ground with the hands and knees in contact with the floor.

b. Place your right hand on the back of your head.

Begin rotating your upper body up and back until you feel mild tension in the midback.

Flexibility 3: Lower-Body Stretch

Place your body in a lunge position with the spine angle straight and the stomach muscles contracted.

Lean forward into the stretch, keeping the same straight back.

Flexibility 4: Shoulder and Midback Stretch

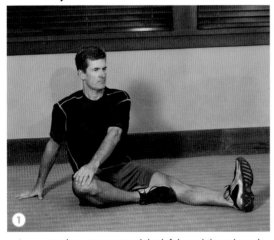

a. In a seated position, extend the left leg while tucking the other leg close to your body.

b. Place the left hand on the right knee and the right hand over the top of the opposite shoulder.

a. Use your hand on your knee as leverage to extend farther into your stretch as you rotate your body toward the folded knee.

b. Continue reaching farther down your back, with your right hand reaching toward the opposite shoulder blade.

Flexibility 5: Lying Glute Stretch

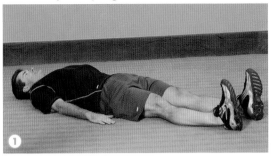

Lie on your back with the legs extended and the arms at your side.

a. Begin by placing the right hand on the left heel.

b. Bring the heel toward the opposite shoulder blade.

Flexibility 6: Lying Back Stretch

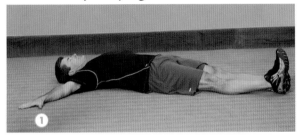

Lie on the floor with your arms and legs extended out.

a. Begin by placing the left leg over the right leg with the knee bent.

b. Place the right hand on the knee joint and allow the bent knee to reach toward the ground.

Out with the Old and in with the New

Fitness training for golf continues to grow and evolve as new information and new research are made public by trainers, physical therapists, physicians, and research analysts. In the not so distant past, sports trainers recommended a brief cardio or stretch session as the most efficient warm-up before the start of a strength training session.

This popular style of warm-up has been replaced by a more progressive series of exercises that focus on increasing mobility while still conferring the benefits of an increased core body temperature and preparing athletes for the work ahead. Often referred to as "movement prep," this series of exercises is designed to keep the body moving through a full range of motion while keeping the intensity light and easy. Here is a great warm-up to start your exercise series in this phase of physical development.

Warm-Up

- **10 body weight squats**. During the second group of five, try lifting your heels off the ground in your lowered position before returning to the top position.

- **10 lunge-to-step-ups**. Proceed into a lunge position, then push off your forward leg and bring it into a knee-high position without touching the ground.

- **10 windmills**. One foot is off the ground, and both arms are extended to your sides. Rotate your body so that one hand reaches toward the opposite foot and return without either foot touching the ground.

- **10 Spiderman push-ups**. Place your body in a push-up position. As you lower your body to the ground, take one knee and bring it toward the same-side shoulder. Repeat with the opposite knee and shoulder.

Sample Technical Phase Workout

Now you're ready for the real workout! A pair of exercises is called a "Superset." In each Superset, do one set of the first exercise, followed immediately by the next (A1 and A2) and then repeat after resting for a minute.

Do the number of repetitions per exercise stated in each program. Do each superset two to three times before moving on to the next, unless instructed otherwise.

GOALS: Decrease body fat, increase strength, increase mobility

Warm-up: 5 to 10 minutes of movement prep

Note: See pages 172 to 175 of the appendix for detailed exercise instructions.

Golf Fitness Workout 1				
Exercise	**Position**	**Sets**	**Reps**	**Rest Interval**
Workout A				
A1. Medicine Ball Back Lunge		2	8 to 10	
A2. Push-up to Arm Lift		2	8	1 minute
B1. Alternating Arm and Leg		2	10	
B2. Glute Lift		2	10	1 minute
Workout B				
A1. Medicine Ball Single-Leg Squat		2	8 to 10	
A2. Windmill		2	6 to 8	1 minute
B1. Squat to Back Row		2	8 to 10	
B2. Elevated Plank with Shoulder Lift		2	8 to 10	1 minute
Stretch for 10 to 15 minutes				

Body Fat Composition and Nutrition

One of the fundamental truths in any sport, including golf, is that excess body fat will affect your performance and energy levels. In the last chapter, we discussed the body fat percentages of elite athletes in different sports. Maybe golf isn't as physically demanding as, say, football or baseball, but that doesn't mean excess body fat won't alter the outcome of your shot-making abilities or jeopardize your energy levels.

Most golfers do not have the body fat levels they need to play their best golf. Although for the majority of golfers this means losing additional body fat, for others it may mean putting on additional muscle weight. Regardless of your specific goals, here is a formula you can use to determine your current basal metabolic rate. This closely approximates the amount of calories your body burns each day based on your height, age, gender, and weight. However, it does not factor in exercise or activity level.

Men:
66 + (6.3 × body weight in lbs.) + (12.9 × height in inches) − (6.8 × age in years)

Women:
655 + (4.3 × weight in lbs.) + (4.7 × height in inches) − (4.7 × age in years)

Once you get your number, be sure to factor in the calories you expend through daily exercise. The following table lists average calories burned for a wide range of sports, depending on an individual's weight.

Calories Burned by Activity

Activity	Approximate Calories Burned per Hour				
	100-lb. Person	125-lb. Person	150-lb. Person	175-lb. Person	200-lb. Person
Aerobics, step: high impact	480	600	720	840	960
Aerobics, step: low impact	336	420	504	588	672
Aerobics: high impact	336	420	504	588	672
Aerobics: low impact	264	330	396	462	528
Bicycling, stationary: moderate	336	420	504	588	672
Bicycling, stationary: vigorous	504	630	756	882	1008
Circuit training: general	384	480	576	672	768
Elliptical training: general	432	540	648	756	864
Golf: carrying clubs	264	330	396	462	528
Golf: using cart	168	210	252	294	336
Mowing lawn: push, hand	264	330	396	462	528
Operating snow blower: walking	216	270	324	378	432
Racquetball: competitive	480	600	720	840	960
Rope jumping	480	600	720	840	960
Rowing, stationary: moderate	336	420	504	588	672
Rowing, stationary: vigorous	408	510	612	714	816
Running: 12 min/mile	384	480	576	672	768
Running: 10 min/mile	480	600	720	840	960
Running: 9 min/mile	528	660	792	924	1056
Running: 8 min/mile	600	750	900	1050	1200

Activity	Approximate Calories Burned per Hour				
	100-lb. Person	125-lb. Person	150-lb. Person	175-lb. Person	200-lb. Person
Running: 7 min/mile	696	870	1044	1218	1392
Sitting: reading or watching television	54	68	81	95	108
Skiing: cross-country	384	480	576	672	768
Skiing: downhill	288	360	432	504	576
Ski machine: general	456	570	684	798	912
Sleeping	30	38	45	53	60
Stair step machine: general	288	360	432	504	576
Stretching, hatha yoga	192	240	288	336	384
Swimming: general	288	360	432	504	576
Swimming: laps, vigorous	480	600	720	840	960
Tai chi	192	240	288	336	384
Tennis: general	336	420	504	588	672
Volleyball: general play	144	180	216	252	288
Walk/jog: jog <10 min.	288	360	432	504	576
Walk: 17 min/mile	192	240	288	336	384
Walk: 15 min/mile	216	270	324	378	432
Walk: 13 min/mile	240	300	360	420	480
Weight lifting: general	144	180	216	252	288
Weight lifting: vigorous	288	360	432	504	576

Your current weight is determined by the ratio of your energy output to your energy input. Your energy output refers to your exercise and activity level, and your input refers to energy in terms of the calories you take in each day. To lose excess body fat, your energy out must exceed your energy in. If your goal is to gain weight, the opposite is true.

These numbers should give you an idea of how to lose or gain weight that is specific to your needs. However, remember that there are other important factors, such as choosing good-quality foods for your energy input. Not only will this help you achieve your body composition goals, it will leave you feeling refreshed and full of energy when you need it most.

To lose body fat, cut your caloric intake by 20 percent daily from the number you just calculated. To gain weight, simply add 20 percent daily to this number. Use regular exercise to expedite your fitness goals.

The technical phase is the appropriate time to make any body fat adjustments. As you get used to a new eating plan with fewer calories, it is well documented that your energy and enthusiasm may be less than stellar. You may find yourself overly distracted with a revised eating plan, and you even may be slightly irritable with the changes required to see quick results. These potential mood swings can be managed effectively during this technical phase, but they can create mental distractions during other phases of competition. Therefore, if you are serious about body fat changes, remain steadfastly focused on your goals during this brief period. Once you hit the pre-comp stage, you will love your new body, new energy, and new swing. This combination makes for winning results.

Here are some nutrition tips that can help you meet your body composition goals:

- Eat high-fiber and low-sugar whole foods such as lean protein (lean beef, chicken, fish, and whey protein), vegetables (broccoli, peppers, and greens), fruit (oranges, apples, strawberries, and blueberries), nuts (almonds, cashews, and walnuts), and whole grains (oatmeal and multigrain bread).

- Eat six small meals daily: three small meals and three snacks.

- Eat fiber-containing foods at all meals in place of processed carbohydrates.

- Stick to dry seasonings only for the first couple of weeks.

- Everyone knows to drink water during this time. Buy a 1-liter bottle of water and set a goal of filling it up two to three times daily.

- Keep your eating plan as simple as possible. When you visit the grocery store, stay along the perimeter, where you will find meats, vegetables, and breads. If you have to ask whether a food is considered "healthy," it probably isn't.

Technical, Mental, and Physical Summary

1. Set specific goals designed to affect the outcome of your game—mental, physical, and technical.
2. Set specific goals for where you want to be with your game in 3 months, 6 months, and 1 year.
3. Begin technical motion drills to improve your swing technique without focusing on the outcome of the shot.
4. Establish a set golf fitness routine with a focus on form and developing proper movement.
5. Use nutrition and exercise to improve body composition.
6. Learn the four P's and think through how you will be applying these principles in your golf game.

Chapter 5
Pre-competition Phase

Called "pre-comp" by those going through the program, this is the phase in which the intensive technical training period begins to pay off with noticeable results. Golfers take what they have worked on in the practice area to the course. Though they are not focused on the score, they take notes on the progress they have made and the areas where there is more work to be done. Golfers in the pre-comp phase are seeing results on the course with improved golf swing technique and improved body composition and fitness levels as well as a renewed and purposeful mental perspective. Let's take our new work to the course and see how it translates!

Some of the key focus areas for the pre-comp phase are course management strategies, relaxation and visualization techniques, getting a feel for distance and sharpening your skills around the green, developing a wider variety of shots, practicing under pressure, tournament preparation, quality practice routines and warm-up procedures, and increasing workout intensity. On-course preparation, planning, and routine take center stage as we transition into the pre-competition arena.

Technical Game Emphasis

We have a newfound confidence in our golf swing and are ready to take our efforts to the next stage. Although we have been learning new shots to add to our arsenal for future competitive rounds, we still are finessing our shot-making options. There are three primary areas of focus in this stage of the game and player development: developing a quality practice routine, creating an effective pre-

shot routine, and improving the ability to "shape shots" for competitive play.

Focus more on tournament preparation and learning how to control the ball. This practice needs to be high intensity and simulate tournament conditions. Accomplish specific tasks during practice and then move on to the next set of tasks.

Let's start with shaping shots. Practice on the range to achieve specific outcomes, for example, 10 draws to a target or 10 fades to a target with short, middle, and long irons.

Draw

To hit a draw:

- Ball position will be back in your stance.

- Body alignment is at the right of the target (feet, knees, toes, and shoulders).

- Swing path is from inside to outside.

Fade

To hit a fade:

- Ball position will be forward in your stance.

- Body alignment is left of the target (feet, knees, toes, and shoulders).

- Swing path is from outside to inside.

Short Game

Short game training is intensive during the pre-comp phase, with specific tasks and pressure drills performed during practice.

Chipping

Here are ways to improve your setup and technique for this shot:

Setup

- Setup mirrors impact position. The feet are narrow, and the stance is slightly open. Grip down on the club with a regular grip, hands forward (butt end points to left hip) and weight favoring the left side. Ball position is back in your stance, which will encourage a descending blow through impact.

- Overall, the body controls the club. Wrists are slightly hinged in the backswing from the weight of the club and unhinged in the downswing. The butt end moves with the chest from impact to finish. The arms and the body control the release of the club to the finish.

- Distance and speed are controlled by the arms, the length of the backswing, and club selection.

- Direction is controlled by alignment, path, and face.

Use this shot for:

- Around the greens

- When you want the ball to run (less spin)

- For different lies

Chipping Side View

Chipping Front View

Right Foot Back Drill

Purpose: Help your clubface come down on a descending angle.

Stand in your normal setup with the right foot back. The sharp angle of the club leans ahead of the ball. Your weight is shifted to the left side.

Club on the Ground Drill

Purpose: To give you a solid hit on the ball without breaking down through impact.

Assume a normal setup position with the club outside your right foot. This will force you to set the club in your backswing, thus allowing the correct angle in your right wrist at impact.

Pitching

Here are ways to improve your setup and technique for this shot:

Setup

- Grip down on the club, making sure you have a light grip so that you can feel the clubhead during the swing. Assume the setup or address position with the stance narrow, the lower body open to the target, and the shoulders square. Feel the impact position (keep a secondary spine tilt), knees toward target, ball position middle (depending on the length of shot and trajectory), arms hanging, hands ahead of the ball, and weight about 60 percent left.

- The swing is a miniature version of the full swing, in which the arms and chest control the motion. The wrists hinge to ensure a good plane and a fluid motion. Accelerate through impact with a follow-through to match the length of the backswing.

- The difference between a chip and a pitch is distance and time in the air. A pitch, unlike a chip shot, has maximum air time and minimum roll, stopping quickly because of the spin on the ball.

- Control distance by width of stance (longer shots need a wider stance), length of backswing (a longer backswing for longer shots), and club selection.

- Direction is controlled by alignment, path, and face.

Use this shot for:

- Distances of 20 to 100 yards to the green

- Recovery shots

Pitching Sequence

Pitching Drills

Target Drill

The key to pitching is distance control. Practice with your different wedges to various targets and make sure you have a way to measure the distance with each club. For example, place targets at 20, 40, 60, and 80 yards. Practice pitching balls to each target.

Right-Arm Swing Drill

Practice some pitch shots with the left arm behind your back. The right-arm swings will help you swing the wedge on plane and control the release with your right side moving through impact.

Towel Drill

Place a golf towel across your chest and under each arm. Use your elbows to hold the towel in place. This drill will help the arms and body stay connected and work together throughout the pitch.

Sand Play

Here are ways to improve your setup and technique for this shot:

Setup

- The most important thing to remember with sand play is to open the face of the club before gripping it. Begin with a wider stance, your weight slightly favoring the left side. The ball is forward in your stance, and your body is open with the knees flexed toward the target. Your hands are positioned low, and your feet are dug into the sand for balance.

- Swing the arms along the body line, keeping the arms and body connected in the backswing. Swing the clubface toward the target in the follow-through, keeping the right heel on the ground. This will allow the body to maintain correct angles during the swing, which will produce a shallow divot and help you control the trajectory and distance of each shot.

- Distance is controlled by alignment. The shorter the shot is, the more open your body and clubface need to be to the target. For longer shots, the body and clubface will be aligned square to the target.

Practice Shots

Uphill Lie

1. Set up with the ball forward in your stance and your body aligned to the right of the target.

2. Grip down on the club. Your body should be parallel to the slope.

Downhill Lie

1. Set up with the ball back in the stance and your body aligned to the left of the target (parallel to the slope).

2. Swing down the slope.

Short Bunker Shot

1. Stand with your body open in relation to the target.

Note: Use a 9 iron for long bunker shots. For buried lies, the face should be closed to 11 o'clock or open with the hands and weight forward (both with a short follow-through).

Bunker Drills

Set specific targets during bunker practice. Set an outcome goal and practice different lies to different targets on the green.

Splash Off a Board

This drill involves placing a board under about 1 inch of sand in the bunker to help you learn bunker technique. Make a smooth swing, feeling a shallow divot, and splash the sand off the board.

9-Iron Drill

Hit with your 9 iron in the bunker to different targets on the green.

Fairway Bunkers

Here are ways to improve your setup and technique for this shot:

Bunker Drill Setup

1. Take your normal setup in the bunker.

2. Grip down on the club with the clubface slightly open.

3. Make sure your weight is slightly on your left side. Ball position should be slightly back in your stance.

The Stroke

a. When taking your backswing, keep your weight centered.

b. Keep your clubface slightly open at setup, as this will help you hit the ball cleanly at impact and control your direction and distance.

Make an 80 percent golf swing and hold your finish.

Lob Shot

Use the log shot when you need that extra trajectory without extra spin once the ball reaches the green. Here are ways to improve your setup and technique for this shot:

Lob Shot Drill

The Stroke

Set the club in your backswing. In the downswing, swing your arms along your body line so that the clubface can pass your hands at impact. During the follow-through, the club will rehinge, staying open, and your knuckles will be facing upward at the finish.

Lob Shot Setup

When you are setting up for a lob shot, your body and clubface are open to the target. Your ball position is forward in your stance, and your weight is 50/50. Your hands are even with the ball, with your spine tilted slightly to the right.

During the pre-comp phase, practice recovery lob shots out of long rough to various targets on the green.

Practice tight lies to different targets.

Putting

The two most important parts of putting are *distance* and *direction*. If you have a constant set-up, it will be easier for you to make a consistant stroke repeatedly, especially under pressure.

Putt Chip Drill

Putting

These techniques are used to give golfers more options and to help them save shots around the green. They also are used when there is a hill or slope between the player and the hole.

Putt Chip Setup

This shot is played with a putting grip.

1. Ball position is under the right eye.
2. Body is aligned open to the target.
3. Grip down on the club with arms at your side.
4. Stance is the same width as your putting stance.
5. Your hands will be in front of the ball for a descending hit.

The Stroke

1. Backswing and follow-through are the same distance.
2. The goal is to hit the ball off the toe of the club.

3-Wood Setup

This shot is played with a putting grip.

a. Ball position is off your right eye.

b. Alignment with your feet is slightly open.

a. Grip down on the club, arms at your side.

b. Stance is the same width as your putting stance.

Putting Drills

Basic Setup

The thumbs sit on top of the grip, and the palms of both hands oppose each other.

Reverse overlap grip to eliminate wrist break and keep the pressure light.

Side View

a. Ball position is forward in the stance, under the left eye. The eye line is over or slightly inside the ball.

b. The hands should be under the shoulders, and the arms should rest on the upper chest, with the elbows close to the side.

Front View

a. Posture is created by the length of the putter, and weight is 50/50.

b. Flex the knee slightly and bend over from the knees and hips.

c. Direction starts with a square clubface at setup.

Putting Drills (continued)

The Stroke

1. The stroke is controlled by the arms and shoulders.

2. The path moves back straight and through for short putts and moves gradually inside for long putts.

3. The putter head will always move on an arc because of the lie of the putter.

4. Distance is controlled by the length of the backswing and the speed of the stroke.

5. Your head and lower body must stay still throughout the stroke to create a consistent path back and through.

The Path Tee Drill

Place tees on the putting path green to help you square the clubface at address and improve the path of the stroke.

Club on the Ground Drill

By placing a club on the ground aimed at the breaking point, you will improve direction and feel for distance in your putting dramatically.

Right-Hand-Only Drill

By placing your left hand behind your back, you will learn how to control your stroke, allowing you to feel the correct release through the ball.

360 Drill

Place balls around the hole from 2 to 8 feet and practice moving in a counterclockwise direction, making sure to adjust your alignment and aim from each angle. This drill will help you read putts and set up correctly to the target.

String Drill

Place a string on the ground to help with preparation and setup. Putting along the string will help maintain your eye line over the ball and improve contact in the middle of the putter.

Practice Routines

Building a Pre-shot Routine

Developing an effective pre-shot routine takes time and practice. In the end, the routine will reflect a system that works for you and that you can embrace for every swing you make, on every course and in every situation. The pre-shot routine is your "constant." It is your routine that puts the whole golf swing and the upcoming shot into motion. Each player will have a different spin on what this should look like and feel like, yet there are certain commonalities in the pre-shot routines of most successful players. Remember, the goal of this routine is to create the right feel in your swing, help you relax, guide your focus, and get the ball to the target. Here are some considerations in developing your own pre-shot routine:

- Each swing should have a specific purpose. Don't think club to ball but rather ball to target!

- Make your pre-shot routine dynamic and alive!

- Begin your routine with a rehearsal swing next to the ball so that you can get a feel of the slope and the lie conditions of the shot.

- Chose a movement that allows you to perform your real swing with the correct tempo and rhythm. You can use a waggle or several short practice swings, for instance.

- Make sure to include some sort of relaxation or visualization technique. For example, Aaron Baddeley always closes his eyes for a second before hitting a shot.

Assess Conditions

Most great players are always collecting vital information on the conditions around them. They know those conditions will affect their club selection and shot selection and ultimately dictate the outcome in terms of their ability to score. Pros think, "Okay, what is my plan here? What do I need to be doing? Where do I want the ball to land?" They're evaluating the direction of the wind and how strongly or lightly it is blowing. By the time they're over the ball, all they're doing is looking at the target, feeling what they want to do, and then pulling the trigger. If you ask anybody who shoots a great score, "What were you thinking?" that golfer will tell you the same thing: "Nothing." All planning and preparing go into the pre-shot routine, and so golfers are free simply to execute once they are at address over the ball.

Practice Like You Play, Play Like You Practice

Proper preparation is one of the hallmarks of this phase. In pre-comp, your attention shifts to 50 percent preparation and 50 percent feel. One of the most challenging areas of the game is to get your practice sessions to transfer to the course. Although you already have taken detailed steps to make this happen by training your mind, body, and swing more purposefully in the previous phases, one of the secret ingredients is to practice the way you play. Here are some scenarios you can practice that resemble real-life scenarios:

- Practice your pre-shot routine with each shot.

- Visualize and then execute the different shots: draws, cuts, knockdowns, lobs, and so on.

- Vary your distances and yardages using your new variety of shots and clubs. Hit it high and watch the ball flight. Hit it low and notice the difference in how the ball behaves with your trajectory.

- Practice various lie positions, including uphill and downhill, ball above your feet and below the feet, poor lies, and so on.

- Practice in varying weather conditions: rain, wind, and other adverse conditions. Remember, adversity builds character.

- Practice putting left to right, right to left, uphill, and downhill.

- Improve your ability to read the greens.

- Practice varying levels of speed with putts.

- Practice a specific putting routine, just as in your course pre-shot routine.

- Apply new breathing techniques and relaxation methods.

- Start each session with a physical warm-up that prepares your body for practice or for play.

- Experiment with different swing tempos and watch the difference in ball spin that is created. A faster tempo creates more spin.

Building a Quality Practice Schedule

One of the most challenging issues facing golfers daily is: "How do I take my practice sessions to the course?" As you are learning through this training process, the best results are achieved by building on a foundation and working your way through this step-by-step periodized approach. Golfers who use this methodical approach to training will find the transition seamless. Quality can be defined as the results of high intention, sincere effort, intelligent direction, and skillful execution.

- Consistency comes from consistent practice.

- The goal is to practice smarter, not harder.

- The goal of practicing is to become a better player, not a better practicer.

- The only way to perform well is to practice well.

- Understand your swing.

- Have an objective/purpose each day at the practice tee or course.

- Work on your drills patiently, feeling the right position.

- Change clubs and targets frequently.

- Practice your routines.

- Practice every part of your game (technical, physical, mental, course management, etc.).

- Imagine yourself in tournament situations. Practice under pressure.

- Be patient.

Mental Game Emphasis

Early in the pre-competition phase, the most significant component from a mental perspective is to assess how the integration of the new techniques and skills developed in the technical phase is working. As an example, if what has been developed in the days or weeks of the technical phase is a takeaway in the swing that incorporates having the wrists set early, getting on the golf course and simply measuring wrist set will be a daily goal. Literally grading oneself on a scale from 1 to 10 on the basis of early wrist set on every shot is a good strategy as opposed to concerning oneself with ball flight, score, or anything related to outcome. This will direct the player's attention to the areas that are of greatest importance, helping him or her achieve greater consistency in the setup, swing, or mental adjustments that he or she has been practicing in a non–golf course setting.

Committing to the Execution of a New Swing

Since you just completed the technical phase, in which you probably integrated some new techniques into your swing, it is only natural and quite common to have some misgivings about how this will transfer to the course. All golfers want to continue in their comfort zones, but at the same time they understand the need for changes in their swings. However, frustration levels sometimes can reach an all-time high as the integration and acceptance of these changes take place.

There are many reasons why a player may have anxiety or reservations about the incorporation of a new swing change. If they are not confident in the swing, players may be concerned they will not hit ball well and it will end up in a hazard, in a bunker, out of bounds, or in some other undesirable place. Others players will end up trying to guide

the ball since they lack faith in their ability to incorporate the new swing change properly. Golfers need to realize that making tentative swings leads to poor results that are not indicative of how the new swing changes could improve their game.

There are two ways to approach a shot, each with two basic results. A swing can be either committed or uncommitted, and the result of any swing can have a positive result or a negative result. This is shown in the following table.

Shot Approaches and Results	
1. Commitment with positive result	2. Commitment with negative result
3. Lack of commitment with positive result	4. Lack of commitment with negative result

Situation 4 is the absolute worst feeling in golf. The player has swung the club tentatively with no commitment to the shot, and the result is a poor shot. The player most likely was thinking about a feared consequence when swinging, and the feared outcome happened anyway. This scenario is a double whammy to one's confidence because of the lack of courage and the poor result.

Situation 3 is only slightly better. The player didn't really commit to the shot but got a positive result anyway. He knows he's "gotten away with one." A player's confidence is not increased when a timid shot is played, even if the ball ends up where the player was hoping it would. This tiny victory feels good in the moment, but it has a negative impact on most players' confidence because they know it wasn't their commitment that created the positive result.

Despite positive results, any shot taken with a lack of commitment will have negative effects on the confidence of a player. In contrast, commitment to a shot inescapably does just the opposite.

Situation 2, in which a player commits to the shot but doesn't get the result she'd like, creates only mild disappointment. Even if the results of the shot are negative, competitive golfers know that by committing to their shots, they've at least given themselves a chance to achieve positive results. By executing a committed swing, they have done all they could to create a positive golf shot. It is easier to accept negative results when you realize that, over time, committing to your swings and putts will produce the positive results you seek.

A committed swing with a negative outcome has a net positive effect on confidence.

Situation 1 is the best feeling in golf. A player has made a fully committed swing at the ball and gets the results he envisioned. When a golfer of any ability sees the positive result of a committed swing, he is reminded of his love for the game. Facing a shot head-on and getting a positive result is one of the biggest confidence boosters.

Our work with golfers of all ages and levels of ability has taught us a lot about the mental side of golf. We have discovered a trend that stretches across the spectrum of golfers, from players in the junior ranks to players on the PGA and LPGA tours. We've found that there are very few times when a golfer is completely comfortable with her game, especially during a tournament.

Players constantly notice when their swing doesn't feel right, when the putter is a little bit off and the putts don't fall, and when the conditions on the course are less than favorable. Even if things seem to be going well, golfers always are plagued with nagging thoughts. If a practice round is played well, perhaps the golfer has peaked too early. If the practice round does not go well, perhaps that trend will continue and the golfer won't play well the next day either. If a player is leading an event, there's the pressure of the other players trying to catch him. If the player is behind in an event, she has the pressure of catching the leader.

Even the best players in the world are never comfortable with every aspect of their game for an extended period. They accept the idea that they will be uncomfortable with something, sometimes several things. Once they acknowledge this, they get on with the business of playing the game with the abilities they have.

Advanced players do not focus on things about which they're uncomfortable. Instead, they direct their concentration to the things that are relevant in that moment. In many cases, they do not wait until they are completely comfortable, because that moment may never arrive. They simply feel the fear and "do it" anyway.

All golfers know the basic truths of the game: There are 18 holes in a round, you can have a maximum of 14 clubs in your bag, and you may not strike another player's ball. As a competitive golfer, there is a mental truth you need to learn in order to advance your game. When you learn to accept being uncomfortable with your game and focus on the things you can control, you will begin to improve and become more successful.

The top professional golfers constantly analyze their games. Along with their successes and great shots, they understand that it is just as important to examine defeat, recognize mistakes, and dissect miscues. Their self-evaluation is methodical and constructively critical. Golfers with less analytical experience are often simply critical, diminishing their confidence, wreaking havoc on their self-image, and inhibiting their ability to integrate lessons and changes effectively into their game.

When asked how it felt to fail over 1,000 times before figuring out how to invent the lightbulb, Edison reportedly responded, "Sir, I never failed. I now know over 1,000 ways how not to create a lightbulb." Golfers would benefit from having an outlook like Edison's. If they play poorly in a tournament or hit some poor shots, they may say to themselves, "Okay, I now know that going for this par-5 in two shots is unrealistic for me. Next time I'll lay up and play to the safer side of the fairway."

Make it a priority to become more constructively critical of yourself, not just critical. If you hit a shot poorly, become comfortable with stating, "Okay, I now know that swing thought or strategy doesn't work well. What adjustments will I make the next time I'm faced with this situation?" Do not focus on the "should haves" or "could haves" of your current round. It is much more beneficial to think about the changes you can institute in the next round.

Trust or Commitment?

Any golfer who has ever taken a lesson probably has been told to "just trust your swing." Any golfer who has ever taken a lesson probably also is struggling with his swing. How do you reconcile the fact that golf can get easier when you are so confident in your game and swing that you can simply trust your swing but you are stuck struggling to gain confidence in your swing and execution?

Virtually all players who have ever played competitive golf experience times when they don't trust one aspect or another of their game. How do you trust that you're going to make this putt if you've previously missed four similar ones? How do you trust that you've made the correct club selection if you've misclubbed on previous holes? The simple answer is that you don't always need trust. When you can't muster complete trust, commitment becomes equally important.

Commitment—to a plan of action, a shot selection, or a putting line—and striking the ball with authority can help develop trust in your game. Committing to your game plan and your swings will help you avoid the mental distraction of second-guessing yourself. It is rare to have complete trust that all shots will turn out well, but the best chance for something good to happen comes when you commit. As the late Payne Stewart was quoted as saying: "It's better to commit to the wrong thing in golf than to be uncommitted to the correct thing."

Here are some tips to help you develop trust in your game by committing to your plans and shots:

- If you are between clubs on a shot, pick one and commit fully to that choice.

- If you aren't sure if a putt breaks 6 inches or 10 inches left to right, choose one and make an authoritative stroke.

- Begin to recognize how many times you've hit a shot without being committed and challenge yourself to pull the trigger only after you've eliminated the other options in your mind.

- You have to look at every decision and every shot as an opportunity to gain feedback about your game. The most accurate feedback comes from shots to which you were fully committed. You can use this feedback to shape adjustments you'd like to try in the future. Without commitment, feedback, and proper adjustments, you may never gain trust in your game no matter how regularly you practice or play.

A Good Mental Warm-Up Is Essential for Peak Performance

Although players may put in time on the driving range to perfect their swings, many do not prepare themselves adequately for each round of golf. There really is no excuse for showing up just a few minutes before a tee time and lacing up your shoes on the first tee box with no thought given to anything other than hitting the ball off the first tee. To prepare properly for a round, you need a warm-up and a plan of action.

A thorough physical warm-up has advantages for all players, not just those hoping to shoot their best score. Proper stretching will raise the core body temperature and loosen muscle groups. Making swings on the range, in the short game area, and on the putting green will help a player prepare for a good round. These techniques prepare your muscles to make the swings you'll need on the course.

A proper warm-up can benefit one's mental preparation for the round as well. In advance of approaching the first tee, there are steps you can take to prepare yourself mentally for the upcoming round. On the way to the course, listen to music with a smooth, slow tempo. That kind of music can help create a mental state that mimics the smooth tempo a golfer should have in his or her golf swing. A smooth tempo for a golf swing is not easily created when a player has been driving like a maniac, talking business on the cell phone, and racing to the tee box.

Anxiety and loss of confidence in competitive players can be caused by a lack of preparation. If a player has a specific warm-up routine before a competition, she can step to the first tee knowing that all the "boxes are checked," reducing first-tee jitters and increasing confidence.

In addition to a warm-up, players benefit from having a goal in mind for the round that day. Ideally, the player will have a process-related goal, not an outcome-related goal. Process goals include things such as "I will be thorough with all my pre-shot routines today," "I will make sure that I have full commitment before each swing I take," and "I will read my putts from at least two sides before I choose my line and speed." These goals emphasize the value of the player's progress, not just the player's score.

Develop and follow a warm-up routine of your own and set goals for each round you play. Adequate preparation can reduce frustration and increase the success and enjoyment of the round.

Creating Positive Pressure

When a player is trying to reach peak performance, his mental training should create "positive pressure," which focuses on minimizing the differences between the practice and competitive environments. The training intensity and purposefulness of amateur and professional golfers alike usually do not match the rigor of an actual competitive environment. To reach peak performance, a player's practice protocols should be fixed, intentional, and very specific.

For example, when practicing chipping just before a competition, a player should change targets after every chip. Changing targets rather than chipping continuously at the same target simulates play during a round of golf. Another chipping drill involves setting a goal for a certain number of chips within a certain radius of the target before moving on to the next drill. To do this, the player must take more time on each shot, preferably completing a full pre-shot routine, and be more deliberate and thorough in

preparation. This drill also allows the player to evaluate his or her progress by counting a tangible number of successes.

Unless a player is working on a specific technical aspect of his or her putting, positive pressure also can be incorporated into putting practice. The player should use a full pre-putt routine, including reading the green, before each practice putt. This mimics and reinforces the way the player might prepare for a putt in competition.

The concept of positive pressure can be traced back to one question: Why would you expect 100 percent results in your practice without proper preparation for each and every putt? Practicing using positive pressure is much more effective than dropping 5 or 10 balls and striking one after another, machine gun–like, in the general direction of a hole. This practice without purpose is immeasurably inefficient and bears little resemblance to a player's routine in competition.

Setting Practice Goals

Many golfers get frustrated when they hit the ball well on the range but can't translate that success to the golf course. Without the guidance of a teaching professional, players tend to look to their on-course behavior, thoughts, and shots for the answer. Frequently, however, the answer lies in their practice routine, not their on-course routine.

It is necessary to hit a lot of golf balls to produce a proficient golf swing. However, few golfers realize that how one practices is as important as how often one practices. Players typically practice by hitting ball after ball on the range with the same club to the same target, over and over again. This is not real golf. The more a player's practice routine resembles her actual on-course routine, the more easily her successes during practice will carry over to the golf course.

Here are four simple steps to incorporate into your practice sessions that will help improve your on-course play:

1. **Change targets frequently**. You rarely will hit two balls in a row to the exact same target during a round. Practice hitting to a different target with each shot whether you are practicing a full swing, pitching, chipping, or bunker shots. Changing targets allows you to think through each shot and execute it as a unique entity—just the way you do it on the course.

2. **Change clubs frequently**. You may not be ready for competitive golf if you regularly hit your 7 iron three or four times in a row on the course. However, this is how many people practice. Changing your club every second or third shot is a good way to approximate your routine on the course.

3. **Use your pre-shot routine more frequently**. Many players use pre-shot routines on the range that are vastly different from the pre-shot routines they use during rounds. These different pre-shot routines create different rhythms, different thinking processes, and different results.

4. **Putt using one ball**. You are not given the luxury of hitting the same putt two or three times on the course, but players drop two or three balls on the practice green and stroke the same putt over and over to the same target. Practice using just one ball. Perform a full read for each practice putt to create a routine that's similar to the one you'd use on the golf course.

Once you have developed a proper golf swing, stop hitting with the same club to the same target over and over on the range. By changing clubs and targets, you're preparing yourself to have a consistent routine on the practice range that will carry over to the golf course.

It takes time for golfers to understand and develop all the fundamentals of their game. Measuring the developmental progress of on-course basics is a challenge if you don't want to use the obvious measurement of your score.

It is essential for golfers to keep a specific purpose in mind when they head out to the golf course. They must have precise accomplishments (or process objectives) to focus on that can determine how much progress is being made. Some examples are listed below:

> ## Conditions
>
> Are all considerations being addressed in determining proper shot selection?
> - Wind speed
> - Wind direction
> - Lie
> - Slope
> - Yardage from the center of the green
> - Hole location
> - Correct choice of club
> - Correct choice of shot

Other Considerations

- Is the player reading the putts thoroughly?
- Are the swing changes being attempted?
- Is the player eating and drinking healthily enough and regularly enough?
- Is the player adhering to the preconceived game plan?
- Is the player playing too quickly or too slowly?
- Are shots being played "one at a time," or is frustration mounting?
- Is a narrow target being selected before a shot is attempted?

Players should select one or two of these items to work on when they play a round. Progress can be tracked on the scorecard by using a hole-by-hole grade with a scale of 1 to 10 or a grade of A to F.

Players who adopt these positive habits will assist their growth and development and ultimately affect their bottom line—their score! The three following tables show sample practice weeks for golfers at different levels.

SAMPLE PRACTICE WEEK: Beginning Golfer

Practice Time	Monday	Tuesday	Wednesday	Thursday	Friday	Saturday	Sunday
1 hour	Range Shaping Shots Putting	Off	Pitching Bunkers Lob shots	Off	Range Body chip Putt chip Short irons	Play golf	Play golf or rest
30 minutes	Fitness training		Fitness training		Fitness training		
20 minutes		Stretching		Stretching		Stretching	

Notes: Weekly practice covers all components of the game. Fitness training will take 1½ hours total and should be circuit-style training so that you can develop strength and get your cardio in each workout. Stretching is for 1 hour total for the week.

SAMPLE PRACTICE WEEK: Intermediate Golfer

Practice Time	Monday	Tuesday	Wednesday	Thursday	Friday	Saturday	Sunday
1 hour	Range	Off	Pitching	Off	Putting	Play golf	Play golf or rest
30 minutes	Shaping shots	Study sport psychology	Bunkers lob shots	Study sport psychology	Putt/chip short irons		
45 minutes	Fitness training		Fitness training		Fitness training		
20 minutes		Stretching		Stretching		Stretching	

Notes: In the intermediate practice schedule, an extra 30 minutes has been added during each week day. This will give golfers an opportunity to further hone specific golf skills.

(actual tour player training schedule)

Practice Time	Monday	Tuesday	Wednesday	Thursday	Friday	Saturday	Sunday
9:30 a.m. to 10:30 a.m.	Range stretching routine	Bunker lob shots	Sport psychology	Range woods and routines	Body chip Putt chip	Cardio/ stretching	Rest
10:30 a.m. to 11:30 a.m.	Short irons drills	Body chip Putt chip	Range practice swings	Bunker lob shots	Putting competition	--	--
11:30 a.m. to 1:00 pm.	Putting technical drills	Range drills	Pitching technical drills	Putting technical drills	Range shaping shots	--	--
1:00 p.m. to 2:00 p.m.	LUNCH	LUNCH	LUNCH	LUNCH	LUNCH	Golf course 18 holes	--
2:30 p.m. to 3:30 p.m.	Fitness training	Golf course 18 holes	Fitness training	Golf course 18 holes	Fitness training	Golf course 18 holes	--
3:30 p.m. to 4:30 p.m.	Fitness training	Golf course 18 holes	Fitness training	Golf course 18 holes	Fitness training	Golf course 18 holes	--
4:30 p.m. to 5:30 p.m.	Bunker lob shots	Golf course 18 holes	Putting technical drills	Golf course 18 holes	Bunker lob shots	Golf course 18 holes	--
5:30 p.m.	--	Golf course 18 holes	--	Golf course 18 holes	--	--	--

Notes: This is the comprehensive training schedule used by an actual player on tour. Golfers can modify this schedule to more closely match their time availability and personal golf performance goals.

Physical Game Emphasis

Up to this point in our physical development process, we have identified our strengths and weaknesses as they relate to our golf swings and have begun building a base level of strength, flexibility, mobility, stamina, and overall fitness. Our golf body is feeling stronger and more mobile, and now we're ready to increase our efforts in terms of volume and intensity as we enter the pre-comp phase of training.

A brief physical preparation as you arrive for practice or play will help prepare your body and mind for the challenges ahead. Just as in the mental and technical sides of golf, the best way to approach this is with a specific plan. This warm-up will be something you do every time you play, forming a routine that you can count

on to create a greater level of consistency in your play year-round.

A Winning Warm-Up

According to a study produced by the *British Journal of Sports Medicine*, a dynamic warm-up can have a significant impact on clubhead speed. In fact, in a study conducted on 20 golfers of matching gender, age, and handicap, it appeared that the clubhead speed of those who performed dynamic warm-up stretches before play was 24 percent greater than the clubhead speed of those who did nothing before play!

There are many ways to conduct a warm-up or stretch routine, and each method can produce good results for a golfer. However, studies have shown that the best way to warm up just before a round of golf is through the use of dynamic stretches. Dynamic stretches are stretches that keep the body in constant motion. These are not stretches that you hold for 10, 20, or even 30 seconds; they are stretches that you hold for no more than 1 to 2 seconds, keeping your body temperature warm with fluid movements. One of the critical reasons golfers use this stretching method is based on research indicating that static stretching (stretch and hold) performed just before an event can decrease strength levels temporarily. This is obviously not the desired outcome for any level of golfer, so be sure to stick with dynamic stretches before play.

On the next 5 pages are some great stretches that hit all the major areas that have an impact on your swing, providing the necessary ingredients to a winning warm-up. Each stretch should be repeated 10 times on each side. Hold each stretch for 1 to 2 seconds while breathing out on exertion.

Lunge with Rotation

Hold a club on your shoulders, with your hands about 6 inches beyond your shoulders. Step forward with the right leg.

Rotate your body into the forward leg. Push off the right leg and return to the start position. Repeat 10 times on each side.

Hamstring-IT Band Standing Stretch

Raise a club over your head, with your hands slightly farther than shoulder width apart.

Cross your left leg over the top of your right leg and bend forward from the hip while keeping a straight back.

Hold a club out in front of your body with the hands on opposite ends of the club. Place your spine in a neutral position. Begin with small swings from left to right.

Gradually increase your range of motion and keep a nice easy rhythm from backswing to downswing.

Advanced Side Stretch

Place both hands on the club slightly farther than shoulder width apart. Place the right foot forward with the knees slightly bent.

Begin by shifting your weight over to the opposite side, stretching both the hip flexors and the obliques.

Midback Standing Stretch

1 Place your feet about shoulder width apart and your body in an athletic position, bending forward from the hip. Place your left hand on the club while resting it against your right thigh. Place your right hand behind the middle of your head.

2 Begin the stretch by rotating your right side back as far as you comfortably can, creating a stretch in the midback and upper shoulder.

Standing Shoulder Rotations

1 Place your feet about shoulder width apart and your body in an athletic position. Hold a club parallel to the ground in one hand.

2 Rotate your right arm so that the face of the club is facing the ground.

3 Rotate in the opposite direction until the shaft is facing the ground.

Standing Shoulder Stretch

Place your left hand on the shaft of the club while your right hand holds the face of the club.

The club is anchored lengthwise across your back shoulder and pulled gently to the front of your body. You will feel slight tension in the top of your shoulder.

All in One Stretch

Start in an athletic body position.

Take one step forward into a deep lunge while placing both hands around your knees. Your back leg stays extended, and your back and spine angle remain intact. Try not to round the back upon leaning forward.

Start this stretch with an athletic body position.

a. Lift one leg and place both hands around the knee, pulling the extended knee close to your body and up toward your chest.

b. Once your balance is established, try lifting the heel of the weight-bearing leg.

A Complete Fitness Program

Until now, your efforts have been focused on building the basics of strength, flexibility, stability, and mobility. Your movement patterns should be engrained at this stage of physical development, and so you can begin increasing your workload as well as the level of difficulty of your exercises. Because golf practice and competitive play can be so time-consuming, the goal here is to choose exercises and programs that will create the greatest challenges in the shortest period. Just as you've heard in regard to the mental and technical sides of the game, quality takes precedence over quantity.

Here is a sample program you can follow during this phase of development:

GOALS: Get strong, get lean, and push yourself (within your available limits)
Warm-up: 5 to 10 minutes of movement prep.
Note: See pages 176–178 of the appendix for detailed exercise instructions.

Golf Fitness Workout 2

Exercise	Position	Sets	Reps	Rest Interval
Workout A				
A1. DB Split Squat		3	8	
A2. Spiderman Push-up		3	8	1 minute
B1. Back Extension on Ball		3	10	
B2. Ball Rollout		3	10	1 minute

(Table continues on page 138)

Workout B

A1. DB Squat and Reach		3	8	
A2. Lateral walk with band		3	10	1 minute
B1. Bar Pull-Ups		3	8	
B2. Medicine Ball Rotations		3	8	1 minute

Stretch for 10 to 15 minutes

Pre-competition Nutrition

By now you should be close to your body composition goals. If you are not, you will stay steadfast with these goals all the way up to competition. Ideally, though, you will be near your competitive weight and body fat goals and begin working on what to eat and drink to fuel a better round of golf.

Golfers can call this a "testing" phase. This is a time when you can try new protein drinks and nutrition bars or different food choices, noticing how your body feels in practice and in play. What works for one person may not work for another. We call this the testing period because we want to find the combinations of nutrition and eating patterns that best complement your game. Remember that once we enter into the competitive phase, we want to know exactly how our bodies operate and under what conditions. Golfers are not looking for something new but for something "tried and true."

Key Elements of the Pre-comp Phase

Technical, Mental, and Physical Summary

1. Prepare quality practice sessions for 1 week and then change as your game develops.
2. Prepare pre-shot routine.
3. Prepare and practice mental and physical warm-up.
4. Try new foods, drinks, and nutrition bars in this stage. Find what works best while you play.
5. Use a new golf fitness program, increasing the difficulty, volume, and intensity.

Chapter 6
Competition Phase

For players whose goals include performing at a high level in tournament play, this phase is what they have been waiting for. In the competition phase there is a strong emphasis on mental and tactical strategies, including ways to recover from mistakes and learning to play with the added pressure of competition. This chapter will suggest only minor mechanical adjustments to the swing and low-impact workouts to limit the risk of injury.

Although some golfers may not have the lofty tournament goals of their peers, this chapter will aid them as their golf training nears its completion. There is not a golfer out there who cannot benefit from the practical on-course advice given during the discussion of the competition phase.

On the golf course, the thought process should be focused on where to hit the ball, not how to hit the ball or how to swing. That's a real challenge for a lot of players.

In competition, great players are focused on the planning and preparation for the shot and the pre-shot routine. Golfers should be immersed in the process of being in the present rather than the past or future.

You will not find great players working on technique in competition; they simply play the game and execute their shots. After a round, they gather information to evaluate what worked and what didn't work, and there may be minor adjustments made for the next competitive round or the next week.

Some players have one simple swing thought they take with them on the course. However, this is not the case with most competitive players. As an example, LPGA player Brittany Lang typically does not have a swing thought. She has a swing "sound" or feel—something she identifies and assimilates as her own unique approach to the ball. For most players, it is contradictory to think and execute at the same time. If you need a swing thought to keep the mind still, the best place to use it is in the pre-shot routine, not in the execution of the shot. If you have prepared properly for the competitive stage of golf, the focus shifts from thought to execution.

Technical Game Emphasis

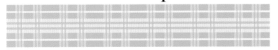

Full-Time Player, Part-Time Caddy

When you come to a competition and have prepared well for the event, you will feel confident in your ability. In your preparation and planning for an event, you should see yourself as 50 percent golfer, 50 percent caddy.

Picture yourself as a caddy for a professional player on tour. How would a caddy prepare? You need to know the yardages. You need to have all the equipment checked. You need to make sure the player has enough balls. You need to have extra clothing for various weather conditions. You also need to have a notebook and a yardage book. You need to know the golf course as intimately as possible—where your player is likely to have difficulties making critical shots, what the greens are like, how difficult the rough is, and which holes may produce the greatest challenges and why.

These are all important considerations in tournament play. The goal of playing in tournaments is to follow the plans you outlined as you moved through your developmental cycle. There should be no surprises that catch you off guard or create stresses you have never encountered before. If you encounter undue stress, you are fully prepared, possessing a deep understanding of what is within your control and what is not. Competition is the time to focus on executing a plan you have worked on for months, so aim high and let it fly!

How to Score When It Matters Most

Playing well and scoring well can be entirely different matters. How many times have you heard a player say something like "I felt very confident with my swing but just didn't see the rewards for my effort" or "I just couldn't sink those putts the way I normally do"?

Players who are most successful in achieving the scores they desire have a list of shared commonalities. Scorers tend to do the following:

- Consistently play at the level of their ability

- Possess a blend of good fundamentals, good attitude, and mental strength

- Prepare well for each tournament

- Possess a winning attitude

- Play golf cleanly and efficiently, without waste

- Know when to take what the golf course gives and when to back off

- Know their strengths and limitations

- Keep their composure under pressure

- Know exactly how far they hit the ball

- Know their confidence level with each club so that they know what to turn to in various situations

Ten Mistakes Amateurs Make

1. Underclubbing
2. Swinging too hard
3. Automatically shooting at the flag
4. Not playing away from trouble
5. Missing the green on the wrong side of the flag
6. Taking too much risk and playing into trouble
7. Trying shots they have never practiced
8. Panicking in the sand or in the tough lies around the greens
9. Misreading the turf, lie, and wind conditions
10. Consistently underreading the break on the greens

Ten Mistakes Pros Make

1. Becoming impatient
2. Playing overaggressively
3. Thinking about swing mechanics on the course
4. Dwelling on the shot already played
5. Thinking about the score and anticipating shots
6. Rushing under pressure
7. Practicing without a purpose
8. Neglecting the short game
9. Overanalyzing on the greens
10. Negatively reacting to poor shots

Tournament Evaluation

After each tournament round, you should be prepared to complete a tournament evaluation like the one shown below. This will help you focus on what went right and what you can improve on next time.

The tournament evaluation can be used as important feedback for upcoming tournaments and help you focus on what is holding you back from playing to your full potential. It focuses not only on what went wrong but on what is working and why.

Tournament Evaluation Form

Date: _____

Event: _____

PREPARATION WEEK

How was your preparation the week before the tournament (long game, short game, mentally and physically)?

_____

_____

Did you feel that the program prepared you for the tournament?

_____

_____

_____

AT THE EVENT

Did you feel confident in your game?

_____

_____

What would you do differently?

_____

_____

_____

Did you play up to your potential?

_____

_____

Scores: _____

Conditions: _____

What did you learn? _____

_____

How can you improve in the next tournament?

_____

_____

Did you keep to your game plan throughout the tournament? _____

_____

Did the best player win? _____

_____

What affected your round most? _____

_____

What area was your strength at the event?

_____

_____

What areas need the most improvement?

_____

_____

POST-PLAY

Did you score well? If not, why not and what would you do differently in your preparation and execution?

_____

_____

How did your practice rounds go? What would you change?

_____

_____

What changes to your practice will you implement on a daily basis?

_____

_____

What changes will you make to the rounds that you play each week in the PGA Tour?

_____

_____

What will help you improve your score?

_____

_____

What about your preparation for the next event? What do you have to do to have the best chance of improving?

_____

_____

Overall thoughts, summary, and commitment to change:

_____

_____

_____

_____

_____

What Do I Do with This Information?

At the end of the next competitive round you play, answer the questions above with complete honesty. Did you stay in the present? Did you focus on the process? Did you see and think about what you *wanted* rather than what you *feared?* Did you remain patient, not allowing your nerves to destroy your thought process?

If you can, break the round down on a hole-by-hole basis and see whether patterns emerge that provide insight into when your mind has a tendency to wander or overanalyze. This information becomes part of a feedback loop that helps you create new goals and areas of focus for the next time out on the course. By breaking down your round from a mental perspective, you will have a better understanding of what you should be working on. Whether it is technique or preparation, you can make the necessary adjustments. Using this information to adjust your game will have a big impact on your performance. It will assist you in differentiating between physical or mechanical flaws and the elements that you feel were affected by mental breakdowns There is a significant difference between making a bogie because you prepared well and simply hit a shot poorly and making a bogie because you hit a quality shot but hadn't taken into account the fact that the wind was blowing in your face. The first example is a physical or mechanical error; the second is a mental error.

Mental Game Emphasis

Listen to almost any interview with the winner of a golf tournament, and some reference will be made to playing "one shot at a time." This sounds like a great idea, but there are very, very few golfers who thoroughly understand this concept, let alone train themselves to play one shot at a time habitually.

The concept of playing one shot at a time can best be explained by a very simple concept diagram:

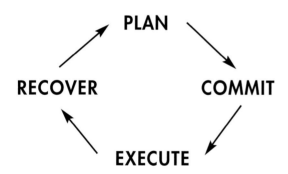

Let's look at each of these phases.

Plan

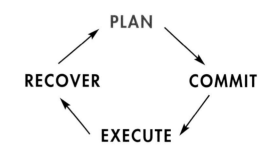

Most golfers will recognize the planning stage as the "pre-shot routine." The benefit of having a well-practiced pre-shot is that it greatly increases the preparation consistency while decreasing the tendencies some players have when feeling stressed, angry, excited, or distracted. In other words, the pre-shot plan reduces the emphasis on *feelings* on the golf course and increases the emphasis on the *doing* part of the game. When players react to their feelings and emotions on the course, what they do in preparation is left somewhat to chance. They may rush, get excruciatingly slow, miss information, make hasty choices, or exhibit a variety of other maladies. The importance of effective planning lies in developing a mental checklist that ensures that you are taking in information comprehensively and that your preparation is optimal regardless of a bad lie or a shot that is off-line. The information that helps determine shot selection typically includes the following:

- Yardage from target (measuring to lay-up area/front edge of green/pin position, etc.)

- Wind (downwind/headwind/crosswind)

- Lie (ball sitting down in rough/perched up on tuft of grass/sitting on short grass)

- Slope (ball above or below feet/upslope or downslope)

- Course conditions (wet/hard/soft)

- Elevation change in shot (uphill or downhill to target)

For advanced players, the specific target, the shape of the shot, and club selection will flow from attention to these details. Too often, for beginning and high-handicap players, too much emphasis is placed on extraneous factors such as what the player's score is, how the playing partners in the group are doing, what the group in front or behind the player is doing in their preparation or pace of play, and who is observing the golfer's shot.

Although at times it is important for players to factor in their score before determining shot selection (e.g., the final two to three holes in a tournament if one is near the top of the leader board), many times score awareness challenges their ability to stay focused on simply hitting a good shot and impels them to strive for a perfect shot. The attempt to make a perfect shot causes most players to tense up, guide the ball, or try to force their swing, which typically results in poor execution. Paradoxically, often the harder one tries to hit a perfect shot, the less likely one is to do so!

Assuming that the player has factored in all the requisite aspects of the shot and has made a good selection ("I like a slight draw with a 9 iron here to land on the front of the green and roll back to the pin placement"), the physical process of the pre-shot begins.

Ensure that this process is purposeful and consistent with your goals for the shot. If you are taking rehearsal swings, make sure there is a purpose for them. If you get behind the ball and look down the line, make sure there is a reason for doing that.

Here is an example of how a player may go about executing a pre-shot routine:

1. Take a full-tempo rehearsal swing standing next to the ball.
2. Get four to five steps behind the ball and look down the line of the shot.

   - Pick a very specific target to which you are hitting the ball.

   - Visualize the shape of the shot flying through the air.

   - Take a big, deep cleansing breath.

   - Pick an intermediate target (12 to 24 inches in front of the ball) to which you will square the clubface.

3. Walk into the shot with your eyes fixed on the intermediate target until the clubface is square to the target and your body is appropriately set up to the club.
4. While waggling the club, stare at the target and glance at the ball.
5. GO!

Commit

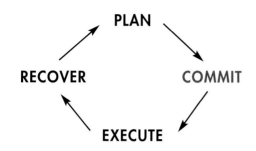

It is very common among sports psychologists to speak of "trusting" one's swing enough to "let it go." Truth be told, very few players—tour players included—trust their swings on a shot-by-shot basis. In fact, distrust in their swings is what confounds even those who have spent countless days hitting thousands of golf balls, countless dollars in golf lessons, and countless hours analyzing their swings on video. Additionally, even for the fortunate few who have learned how to trust their swings, there regularly remains a high level of distrust in their shot selection or in the idea that they are going to get the outcome they desire from a shot.

Therefore, an important distinction should be drawn between *commitment* and *trust*. Trusting one's swing and shot selection is always a desirable quality in a golfer. However, it is not an essential ingredient in outstanding golf. For example, if a player is between clubs, the dialogue might be something like this: "Is this a little 7 iron or a hard 8?" As this internal dialogue continues, the player might conclude, "I'm going to go with the little 7 iron." What usually happens in this situation is that by the time the player is standing at address, ready to strike the ball, he is still thinking about whether the 7 or the 8 was the "right"

choice. Often the player will stay somewhat ambivalent about the choice and pull the trigger anyway. What happens far too frequently is that the player will make a tentative pass at the ball and not hit a quality shot, thus "confirming" that the 7 iron was the "wrong" play. The player might have been able to make a better swing on the ball (with either a 7 or an 8 iron!) if he had been fully committed to his choice. This is what the late Payne Stewart was referring to when he stated that it is better to be committed to the wrong choice than uncommitted to the correct one.

When a golfer is reading a putt, from one side it looks like it breaks two cups right to left, but from the other it seems to break one cup. Which one is "right"? To which read will the player commit? It is difficult to guarantee that either read is correct.

However, any golfer should rest assured that if she *commits* to either a one- or a two-cup break, the putt will be struck with authority rather than being jabbed tentatively, giving it a much better chance of going in the hole.

Ultimately, when in doubt, making a full commitment gives a player a greater chance of success than being hesitant can.

Execute

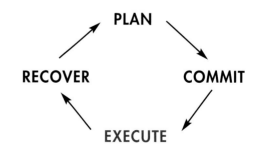

The whole purpose of this chapter is to help players recognize that effective execution in golf is enhanced greatly by adequate recovery from the previous shot, a thorough plan for the next shot, and complete commitment to the plan before swinging the club or putter.

Despite all the time and attention paid to proper swing and stroke technique, it is interesting how players react when they recognize that in the course of a 4- to 5-hour round of golf, the actual "execution" or ball-striking phase of the round takes approximately 15 minutes (assuming 90 strokes, each taking around 10 seconds to execute from setup to ball strike).

Obviously, without adequate ball-striking skills and technique, golfers typically will not play well. However, golfers also will not play up to their potential if they do not understand, practice, and implement the one-shot-at-a-time model. All the emphasis placed on learning how to execute well will not by itself help a player perform well.

Recover

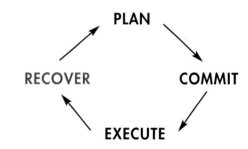

In many golf instruction books and on television golf programs, a considerable amount of attention has been paid to the benefits of a solid and consistent pre-shot routine. Players, instructors, and mental coaches extol the virtues of and the advantages gained from solid preparation before executing the next golf shot. Less attention has been given to an equally important component: the "post-shot," or recovery, phase.

Most players' recovery is left to happenstance and consists of a long string of expletives and/or self-deprecating statements except for the occasional verbal pat on the back if one happens to hit a good shot. While anger and frustration are natural, normal reactions to a poorly hit shot or incidence of bad luck, an important question to ask is, "Are your anger and frustration mobilizing you to action, or are you allowing them to immobilize you?" More simply put: "What are you doing about it?" The best players in the game get angry in virtually every round they play, *but they recover from their anger and frustration quickly and move on to the next shot.* How do they do this? The number-one answer is that they train themselves to monitor their self-talk. Allow yourself a couple of seconds for your initial emotional reaction, then check your self-talk. In checking for helpful self-talk, here is a simple guide: speak to yourself as you would want your caddie or instructor to speak to you. What would it be like if after you hit a poor shot or missed an easy putt, your caddy or instructor said to you, "That shot was horrible" or "What's wrong with you?" or "You can't make a putt today"? I suspect that you quickly would consider firing that person, as his feedback was negative and unhelpful. Instead, you would prefer to hear a phrase such as "Come on, you're okay," "Let's make the next one," "Stay focused on the next shot," or "Better preparation next time."

In addition to self-talk management, another strategy in post-round analysis is to monitor whether attention is being paid to things that are controllable or things that are uncontrollable. Some of the things over which you have control as a player are the following:

- Gathering of preparation elements (wind check, yardage numbers, etc.)

- Commitment to a game plan

- Commitment to a line of putt or target of shot

- Commitment to a specific shot selection

- Clarity of the picture in your head before you hit the ball

- Tempo

An honest assessment of these elements can be helpful and constructive. It is far better to spend precious post-shot time evaluating and improving those things over which you have control than to waste time and energy on those things over which you have no control, such as the outcome of a shot, a bad bounce, and poor swing execution. You may have some influence over these things, but you do not have complete control over them. Recognize this fact and discipline yourself to be purposeful about letting this stuff go. If you don't, you run the risk of engaging in tangential thinking that sidetracks you from the one-shot-at-a-time model.

Another tip that has proved helpful is to take a full-tempo swing in post-shot recovery if you don't like the way the previous swing, chip, or putt felt. Take care not to overthink it or focus on the technical elements. This strategy is valuable in that it reinforces a better feel than you had with the previous swing before you put the club back in the bag. Thus, the last swing with every club in your bag was one that you liked!

Constructive post-shot recovery also involves maintaining positive, strong body language. Champion golfers look like champions most of the time they are on the course, independently of how they are playing or where they are on the leader board. Walking with your head upright and striding purposefully (but not sprinting!) send a message to yourself and your opponents that you are someone to be reckoned with on the course at all times. Many great athletes in a variety of sports have spoken of the benefits of acting "as if" everything is okay even if the circumstances around them don't indicate that.

The other side of this coin is to respond with negative body language: head down, arms folded, walking either too quickly or too slowly. Behaviors such as these create a physiological barrier to being tension-free and a psychological barrier to focusing on the next shot with full attention and a positive frame of reference. Also, in match play situations, this body language conveys to your opponent that you are insecure or distracted, and that has the potential to give your opponent a surge of confidence.

Take a Break

Another key element of the one-shot model is the necessity to detach oneself mentally from the round between shots. There are very few—if any—players capable of sustaining concentration and focus for 4 hours or more without a break. Thus, it is essential to disengage mentally from the round in order to stay sharp. The challenge is to take this break at the optimal times in your one-shot process. Make sure that you allow yourself a break only when recovery is complete or when your plan is complete. Don't take a break between commitment and execution or between execution and recovery.

Here are some suggestions about what to do when detaching from the round:

- Pay attention to the nature/scenery around you.

- Chat with your caddy or playing partner or partners.

- Hum or sing a song in your head.

- Replay scenes in your head from movies or television shows you've enjoyed.

Having a fresh mind for the next shot is necessary to be up to the challenge of playing one shot at a time!

The Traits of a Champion Begin with Perseverance

What is one of the most significant attributes that separates the champions from everyone else? It's not hand-eye coordination, it's not strength or speed, and it is not length off the tee. What separates the trophy winners from the rest is *perseverance*.

To persevere in the face of all obstacles to one's development as a golfer is the hallmark of a premier player. To recognize that every failure is an opportunity to learn, to remember the saying "Sometimes success is just a matter of hanging on," to try and try again—*this* is perseverance.

Perseverance requires discipline and patience. The player makes a plan, sticks with the plan, and minimizes distraction. This intentional process is applied on a consistent basis regardless of adversity or challenges. In a large sense, this discipline helps the player stay focused on his or her long-term development. In a smaller sense, it assists the player in getting back on track in the middle of a round, when things aren't going his or her way.

One of the best-known stories of perseverance in golf is Phil Mickelson's quest for a major victory. After 12 years on the PGA Tour, Phil was considered the greatest player without a major crown. Despite tremendous talent and popularity, Phil was 0 for 42 in that arena. Whenever questioned about the subject, Phil would stick to his "my time will come" mantra. In 2004, in one of the most exciting major victories at Augusta, Phil Mickelson and Ernie Els battled it out for the green jacket on the back nine. He was asked if he had ever imagined a career without a major win. "I had never thought about that," Mickelson said. He paused a beat and with a big grin added, "Nor do I have to."

Understanding the Post-shot Routine

The idea of utilizing a thorough and consistent post-shot routine when playing golf is misunderstood by the majority of players on the course. The routine is to be carried out subsequent to virtually every shot that you hit on the golf course, without regard to the shot's outcome.

For most players, when they have hit a shot that didn't end up the way they would have liked, the time immediately after hitting the ball often is spent in frustration and anger, thinking about how poorly the ball was hit. Additional time typically is wasted trying desperately to figure out what went wrong with the previous swing, chip, or putt. It is critical that you take time to reinforce mentally the feel and sight of the good shot you just hit or to rehearse the same shot if you've hit it poorly.

As an example, you have 150 yards to the pin and you select the 7 iron to give you the best chance of a good shot. If you swing that 7 iron well, watch the full flight of the ball, reinforce within yourself how that felt, and replay the trajectory of the shot. Conversely, if you chunk the ball

only 80 yards, rather than immediately going into a checklist of what you must have done wrong and why your swing didn't work well, reswing the club at full tempo until you get a good feel.

This will imbed in your mind the capacity to swing this club well and also serve as a foundation for the next time you attempt a similar shot. The last swing you took with a club will be the swing that is freshest in your muscles and your memory. When the 7 iron goes back into the bag after you have swung it well, regardless of how the shot turned out, you're likely to feel more confident about that club when you select it for a shot later in the round. The last swing of every club in your bag should be the one that feels good and produces this confidence.

When you reswing the club after a poor shot, be sure that the purpose of the reswing is to establish a swing that feels good. Do not reswing the club while thinking about a swing correction. Swing analysis should be done in the practice area, ideally with a teaching professional's guidance, not on your own on the golf course. Most amateur golfers are not equipped to analyze why or how a shot went wrong. Seemingly random guesses are made about what was wrong with the swing in question, and usually there is an attempt to fix something that never needed fixing in the first place. This on-course guessing creates a string of introduced swing flaws that can unravel a player's swing in the course of a single round.

If you focus on having a successful shot and visualize that shot in your reswing, you're more likely to swing the club fluidly. Let your body do what you've been training it to do on the practice range!

To summarize:

- If you hit a good shot, take time to reinforce the feel and sight of the shot mentally. Having this positive mental image will help you visualize this type of shot the next time you're in a similar situation.

- If you hit a shot poorly, take time to rehearse the same shot. Make sure the most recent swing you've taken with your club was one about which you felt confident. Keep the positive images and muscle memories fresh in your mind and body.

Creating Positive Pressure

Golfers of all abilities commonly take inventory of their game immediately before starting a round: "How am I hitting my irons today?" "What's the driver doing?" "How is my putter feeling in my hand?" "How is my touch around the chipping greens?" Players in a competition can get into a continuous cycle of evaluation of their skills during the round. Minor adjustments can be based on this analysis, and that can be beneficial. However, it is important for players to not go too far in their evaluations before and during a competitive round to avoid misinterpreting the information they are evaluating.

To prevent misinterpretation of their gathered information, players must understand the difference between two concepts: *trait* and *state*. A trait is a relatively permanent characteristic that commonly refers to one's personality or behavior. A person's traits appear or occur on a very regular basis with or without conscious effort. State is related to an immediate but temporary condition, such as one's state of mind. A state is experienced in the immediate present.

What do traits and states have to do with golf? Most golfers, even top professionals, pay too much attention to the immediate state of their game and not enough attention to their golfing traits. The moment their swing feels off or they start missing putts, players tend to focus on the current state of their game: "My putter's off today." "Something is wrong with my driver." "I'm chunking everything with my wedges." There are two areas of concern when golfers focus too intently on the state of their game:

1. Players overanalyze their game, becoming more mechanical and less fluid.
2. Players don't remind themselves of their traits as a good putter, ball driver, or ball striker, and that undermines their sense of confidence.

Let's use an example. If you miss a few putts during a round, do not pay too much attention to the state of your putting. It is much more productive to remember your traits as a putter: "I make putts all the time in practice; they'll start to fall." "I've been working hard on my putting and hit some great putts that just didn't go in. Stay patient." "I'm a good player. Relax and get to the next shot, and things will be fine."

If you hit a few bad shots in a round and start to lose your confidence, remember the practice you have put in to develop your game, your ability to execute good shots, and previous rounds in which your game wasn't going well but things turned out well enough. Emphasizing the traits of your game can boost your confidence when you are dissatisfied with your most recent performance on the course.

Physical Game Emphasis

One of the questions most frequently asked among competitive players worldwide is, "How should my fitness routine change during tournament rounds?" Did you know that Phil Mickelson, Annika Sörenstam, and Mike Weir all train while traveling on tour and before almost every major event? Why do they train the morning of the Masters, the PGA Championship, and the U.S. Open?

Training regularly is a vital part of helping them stay fit. If they normally train every Thursday and it so happens that the Masters is played on a Thursday, is that an excuse to interrupt the routine? Being consistent is a very important part of a golf routine and mind-set. In fact, many

professional golfers would argue that it is disruptive not to work out as scheduled.

The goal of fitness in the competitive phase is to maintain the strength, mobility, and flexibility gains you made in the previous stages. Although golfers in the competitive stage focus on body maintenance, that does not mean they stop working out. In fact, workout consistency plays a vital role in staying in shape throughout the competitive season. For some golfers, competition is fleeting and may take place only a couple of times each year. For others, the competitive season can last anywhere from 3 months to 9 months, depending on the level of play. Imagine working hard for several months of the year only to stop exercising altogether. Most golfers enjoy the benefits of all their hard physical work throughout the season. However, those benefits will fade away if a golfer doesn't do the work required to stay in shape for the entire season.

What changes are made in fitness training during the competitive season? The routine does not change, but the intensity does. This means you may not work out as long or as hard, but most seasoned players will work out as planned. Once a routine is established, it is important to follow it, even during competitive events. By decreasing intensity in workouts, a golfer can take a nice mental and physical break to focus more closely on the technical elements of his or her game.

I go to the gym every morning, it doesn't matter what day it is, if I'm playing golf. Mostly Mondays I take off, but like today, I was in the gym at 7:00 and knowing that I have an hour workout before I go out there. Besides that, I give myself an hour before I tee off on the range, maybe 20 minutes on the putting green. Just the same thing that everybody else does, I've been doing that forever.

—Vijay Singh

Golf Fitness Routine in a Competitive Phase

Many, if not all, of the exercises in the competitive phase are the same exercises we have performed in the past. These are exercises the body knows how to perform. Because your body has grown accustomed to working out and being fit, you feel strong, healthy, and energetic. You know that when you work out, you feel stronger on the course both physically and mentally.

Golfers are not looking to lift weights in an effort to set a personal best record or push themselves beyond their current capacity in this stage. Workouts are performed with slightly less intensity and are likely to be modified so that they can be performed on the road regardless of where the golfer stays. Here's a sample workout for the road in the competitive phase. As in previous stages, the exercises are performed in a "Superset" fashion.

Goals: Maintain fitness levels, including strength and flexibility.

Warm-up: 5 to 10 minutes of movement prep

Note: See pages 179 to 181 of the Appendix for detailed exercise instructions.

Exercise	Position	Sets	Reps	Rest Interval
Workout A				
A1. Split Squat		2	10	
A2. Push-up to Hand Cross		2	6	1 minute
B1. Lateral Walk with Band		2	10	
B2. Fit Band Cross-Body Rotation (Gym: use weight pulley stack)		2	10	1 minute

	Workout B			
A1. Single Leg Reach (Gym: DB Single Leg Reach)		2	8	
A2. Cross-Body Plank		2	10	1 minute
B1. Fit Band Row (Gym: DB Row)		2	10	
B2. Side Plank		2	20 seconds	1 minute
	Stretch for 10 to 15 minutes			

Golf Nutrition in a Competitive Phase

If you have followed your plan exactly as intended in the assessment and technical phases, your body fat is right on target and you are happy with the way you look and feel. This is not the time to focus on body fat changes, because your energy levels may suffer.

All our attention and focus shifts to golf-specific nutrition. These are foods and a planned way of eating that allow golfers to play and think their best on the course. Golf-specific meals and snacks typically are built around the sound principles of performance-based eating. Here are some of the key rules of performance nutrition while competing:

1. Preparation is key. Once you're on the road, you are at the mercy of chain restaurants, unexpected schedule changes, long hours of travel, and extended waiting times between events. Competitive players always call ahead and find a hotel with a gym and a refrigerator or access to a cooler so that they can stock their own snacks or meals.

2. Always travel with some snacks that don't melt or need to be refrigerated and that will fit in your golf bag without hassle. What makes the short list? Try peanut butter pretzels, handmade trail mix, and a dry mix of your favorite meal-replacement drink. Water might be your only option to keep things healthy in preparing your mix. Ideally, you want to eat whole foods with high fiber, but you can't always control some of these variables. Always have a backup plan so that you can stick to your eating schedule.

3. Have an eating plan. Once you know where you will stay, what amenities are available, and your designated tee times, you can plan your meals. You may have a favorite restaurant or two in the local area, or you may plan on eating at the event. You can plan an extra stop at a local market and place your golf snacks in a small handheld insulated bag for your round. Follow your eating plan and don't get sidetracked by a better offer as the cart drives by or as you see some tempting items at the turn.

When they are playing, most golfers select food choices from the glycemic index. A complete list is available at www.glycemicindex.com. The glycemic index refers to the relative degree to which a person's blood sugar increases after the consumption of different foods. Carbohydrates are categorized by the rate at which they release sugar into the bloodstream. Most carbohydrates are categorized as high-release (quick), midrelease (medium), or low-release (slow). Can you guess which foods help produce champions and which foods can add strokes to your scorecard?

By using slow-release foods before and throughout your round, you have the best opportunity to optimize your performance on the course. Slow-release foods supply the body with a steady release of energy and allow golfers to maintain their mental focus. Here's a look at how some popular slow-release and quick-release foods are categorized.

Low (Slow) Release

Oatmeal
Apples, oranges, pears, strawberries
Multigrain bread
Cashew nuts
Fruit and nut mix
All-bran cereal
Yogurt
Raw carrots
Soy milk banana smoothie
Wheat tortilla

High (Quick) Release

Cream of wheat
Watermelon, pineapple
Bagel, white
Raisins
Cranberry juice cocktail
Whole-grain, corn-bran, and corn cereals
Fruit bars
Potatoes
Gatorade

Here are some performance-based snacks and minimeals, categorized by all the variables that will affect your ability to prepare for an upcoming competitive round.

Access to a Refrigerator or Freezer

Frozen grapes or strawberries
String cheese with a handful of whole-wheat crackers
Lean roast beef or turkey wrap with a small amount of ranch dressing
Sliced apples or pears with low-fat cheese wedges
Veggie wrap with almonds
Seven-grain Belgian waffle with a handful of almonds or cashews
Peanut butter wrap with grapes or sliced bananas
Protein bar with sliced apples
One-half whole-wheat bagel, pita bread, or high-fiber tortillas with lean meat slices
Pita bread with low-fat cottage cheese
Banana with peanut butter or soy nut butter
Whole-wheat tortilla wrap with black beans and salsa
Yogurt with raisins and almonds
Whole-wheat tortilla with chocolate-hazelnut spread and sliced bananas

No Access to a Refrigerator or Freezer

Peanut butter–filled pretzels

Handful of trail mix (homemade preferred to keep sodium content down)

Protein bar

Dry protein/carbohydrate meal-replacement mix (just add water)

It is common among competitive golfers to ask, "How many strokes will I save if I use the principles of performance-based nutrition?" Although it is difficult to know whether it is one stroke, two strokes, or perhaps more, we know that a stroke you save could be the difference between first place and second place. When you eat, think, and train like a champion, you instantly remove all the barriers and excuses for not winning and give yourself an opportunity for success.

Key Elements of the Competitive Phase
Technical, Mental, and Physical Summary

1. Use the "one-shot-at-a-time" model.
2. Integrate a post-shot routine.
3. Engage in a preparation and planning thought process during competition, not a technical thought process.
4. Continue your golf fitness program with decreased intensity and volume of work.
5. Use a performance-based nutrition plan.
6. Remember you are part caddy, part player, so stay prepared.

Chapter 7

Active Rest and Regeneration Phase

Even though golfers may not experience the intense physical demands placed on those who play other sports, they still need rest and regeneration to guarantee continued success. This chapter covers what a golfer in this training program should do on off-days and provides ways to be productive without using excess energy. After you accomplish a goal, it is natural to experience a letdown, or a period of unwinding and reflection on the things you failed to accomplish. A golfer must know how to recognize it and limit its impact so that the lull in activity does not become permanent. This is also the phase in which an evaluation is made of what went well during the training program and what can be improved for the next time.

Use the active rest period as a time of reflection in which you have the opportunity to evaluate past performance and accomplishments. Golfers can begin the goal-setting process all over again by asking pertinent questions such as "How will I do things differently next season?" and "What worked to my advantage, and what new weaknesses did I uncover?"

Assessment Phase

Now you'll be ready to move back to the assessment phase, where you will be able to take another objective view of your performance and continue the process of developing as a player.

Technical Game Emphasis

Think of the active rest period of your periodization program as a continuous feedback loop. Remember that in the pre-competition phase you were taking notes about the way you played. Now it's time to begin the reevaluation process.

This is a great time to put your clubs aside and reflect with a clear perspective on what you've done and where you need to improve. It may be a time of putting the clubs down and not touching them for a couple of days so that when you pick them up again, you can get your feel back with an uncluttered mind. Whether you take off a week, two weeks, or just a day or two, it's important to go through the process of letting go. Your clubs will be there when you return!

Mental Game Emphasis

Active rest is a time for a player to get away from the game and/or competing. It basically is an opportunity to shut down psychologically and physically from the game. Active rest is not lying on the couch for a week, and it's definitely not playing golf. It typically involves complete detachment from the game to the degree that a player will allow while engaging in an activity that provides some kind of mental and physical stimulation, such as swimming or hiking.

From a mental perspective, one of the greatest problems in the active rest period is that a lot of players, particularly high-quality players, feel worried that if they lay off for any amount of time, their game is going to suffer. It is a challenge for most intense, competitive players to trust in the proven idea that rest is an essential part of the training process. With so much emphasis on working harder than the next player and not letting other players "pass you by," it may be difficult to set the clubs down for a period of time. This segment of time, which allows for the player to "recharge the batteries," is crucial to creating an internal environment that prepares the player for the next cycle.

Physical Game Emphasis

Rest, relaxation, and rejuvenation are a critical part of every golfer's long-term success. Depending on the length of the competitive season, a golfer deserves some time to unwind and not place any more stress on the body or the mind.

Fitness for Life

Physical fitness training was never designed for the specific needs of playing golf. Of course, your fitness level can play a big role in your playing performance, but it's important to look at the big picture. When you embrace fitness for all it has to offer you in life, you are likely to stay with it. You may love the extra energy you feel when you work out. You may enjoy feeling the freedom of movement that follows a stretch session or the feeling of accomplishment you get when

you push your body a little beyond where you thought it could go.

A fit body is a personal gift—it is something no one can give you but which you can give yourself. It helps keep injuries at bay, allows you to perform movements well past your prime, and makes you feel healthy during your short time here on earth. Fitness also can create an attitude that can make you feel invincible on the tee and nerveless on the greens. Remember Annika Sörenstam's famous debut on the PGA Tour at the Colonial? She credited her physical strength with giving her the mental fortitude to handle all the pressure that came with the media circus and public interest.

In active rest, it is important to allow your body time to recover. During the season there are ample opportunities to create stresses on the body, and recovery is a natural component of development. Some see it as taking a step back so that you can move two or three steps forward in the preseason. Recovery and rest can consist of simple changes such as reducing your workout schedule from 5 days to 2 or 3. It also can mean changing from your daily gym workouts that are geared toward golf-specific movement patterns to an overall fitness program.

Cross-training is one of the best ways to stay in shape and take an active break from the golf season. Try going for a hike with family or friends, skiing in the off-season, or going for a bike ride. Rest doesn't have to be "absolute." Just reduce your intensity and the nature of your activities and try to take the focus off having a purpose for exercising. In other words, enjoy fitness for what it does for you and just relax and enjoy the moments you've worked so hard for.

The Cycle Repeats Itself

Golf training is an endless cycle of continual improvement when a golfer adopts the periodized approach to training. The cycle began with breaking down all elements of the game so that each golfer could better understand his or her swing, fitness level, and ability to process critical information to make appropriate course management decisions.

Then each golfer created a blueprint for future development by focusing on technique, feel, and body motion. That knowledge expanded to include physical and mental warm-up routines to better prepare a golfer's body. In this phase golfers practiced "shaping shots" and explored their potential on the course.

Then they were ready to play. Golfers took copious notes during and after tournament rounds so that they could gather enough information to get better acquainted with themselves as competitive players of the game. The notebook was taken back to the assessment phase when the competition season ended so that they could use it as starting information on which to improve. Last but not least, golfers rested and took time to reflect on the agony of defeat and the thrills of glory.

Today golfers have the opportunity to improve every facet of their game, their bodies, and their minds in the most efficient manner. A periodized approach to golf training is the secret among touring pros around the world, and now it is your secret too!

Key Elements of the Active Rest/Regeneration Phase
Technical, Mental, and Physical Summary

1. Rest, relax, and rejuvenate your mind and body.
2. Cross-train to remain active even while "resting."
3. Begin a period of reflecting on what worked, what didn't work, and what you'll do differently next season as a result.
4. Repeat the cycle of assessment–technical–pre-comp–competition–active rest.

APPENDIX

Pre-round Goal Self-Assessment

Player Name: _____   _____
_____

Date of Round: _____

1. What are my top three goals for golf?
_____
_____
_____
_____
_____

2. What are my long-term goals in golf? (Up to 1 year)
_____
_____
_____
_____

3. What are my short-term goals in golf? (Up to 6 months)
_____
_____
_____

4. What are my immediate process goals?
Technical (swing mechanics):
a. _____

zz _____
_____

Mental:
a. _____

b. _____

Physical:
a. _____

b. _____

5. Am I committed to work 100 percent toward my goals? Yes/no; why: _____
_____
_____

Post-round Self-Analysis

Player Name: _____

Date of Round: _____

Course Name: _____

Score: _____

1. Strengths during the round:
Technical (swing mechanics):

a. _____

b. _____

Mental: _____

a. _____

b. _____

Physical: _____

a. _____

b. _____

2. Opportunities for improvement during the round: _____

Technical (swing mechanics): _____

a. _____

b. _____

Mental: _____

a. _____

b. _____

Physical: _____

a. _____

_____

b. _____

_____

3. I followed my game plan _____ percent of the time during the round.

4. I made the following adjustments during the round:

_____

_____

_____

_____

5. What effect did those adjustments have on my round?

_____

_____

_____

6. Did I play to my potential?

YES _____ NO _____

_____

7. Did I let an outside opponent or situation affect my performance?

YES _____ NO _____

_____

8. If I did not play well: what can I do differently to play up to my potential?

_____

_____

_____

9. If I played well: how can I improve my performance during my next round?

_____

_____

_____

Fitness Routine Exercise Descriptions

> **Golf Fitness Workout 1**
>
> **Goals:** Decrease body fat, increase strength, increase mobility
>
> **Warm-up:** 5 to 10 minutes of movement prep
>
> **After workout:** Stretch for 10 to 15 minutes

Workout A

A1. Medicine Ball Back Lunge

- Stand with good posture and your feet shoulder width apart. Arms should reach forward, fully extended, holding the medicine ball.

- Take one step backward and proceed to lower your body into a lunge position. Lower your body until your back knee approaches but does not touch the ground.

- Push off with your rear foot and return to the start position. Be sure to keep the alignment of your feet so that your forward knee is pointed over your second toe and your knee does not extend over your foot. Keep your body in good posture with shoulders back and down, and do not lean forward into the lunge.

A2. Push-up to Arm Lift

- Place both hands on top of a bench with your feet extended. Make sure your body is in one straight line from the shoulders to the ankles. Hold your stomach muscles in tight.

- Lower your body until your chest is within a few inches of the bench.

- Raise your body back up to the start position and repeat.

B1. Alternating Arm and Leg

- Lie on your back with knees bent and arms together and lifted above your chest.

- Tighten the abdominal muscles and slightly squeeze the buttocks to press the small of the lower back into the floor.

- Alternate arm and leg movements together so that the left arm is slowly extended overhead while the left leg is lifted.

- Repeat with the opposite leg and arm. Always keep your back flat against the floor.

B2. Glute Lift

- Lie down on the floor on your back. Bend your knees and place your hands at your side.

- Lift your toes off the ground with the heels remaining. Engage your abdominals and glutes and then slowly lift your hips off the ground until your body forms a diagonal from your knees to your shoulders. Slowly lower your hips back down, then repeat. Don't let the glutes touch the ground while you perform repetitions.

Workout B

A1. Medicine Ball Single-Leg Squat

- Balance yourself on one leg with the opposite leg extended behind you. Hold a medicine ball in front of you with your arms slightly extended.

- Begin the movement by sitting back and down into a squat. Go only as low as you can while controlling the movement. Push through your heels to return to the start position.

- Perform a separate set for each side.

A2. Windmill

- Balance on one leg while keeping both knees slightly flexed. Reach both arms straight out to your side.

- Begin the movement by bending forward from the hip, raising your lifted leg behind you.

- Slowly rotate your entire trunk and upper body so that one hand touches the same-side foot while the other arm rotates up toward the ceiling.

- Hold and then return your body to the start position.

- Alternate legs and the direction you rotate within the set.

B1. Squat to Back Row

- Stand with your feet shoulder width apart and knees flexed into a partial squat position. Place one end of a fitness band around an object a few feet away while you hold the other end with your palm facing down.

- To begin, push through your heels to move up and out of the squat position and rotate your wrist 180 degrees as you pull the band back into a row. The palm will be facing up while at the top of the row position. The shoulders should remain down and back, and you should feel this in the back of your shoulders and in your back muscles.

- Slowly release the tension and return to the start position, rotating your wrist back so that the palm faces the floor again.

B2. Elevated Plank with Shoulder Lift

- Place dumbbell in one hand while resting your shoulder on the side of a chair or bench. Make sure your elbow is directly underneath your shoulder. Your legs are stacked on top of each other and extended straight out to the side. Focus on good posture with the abs contracted.

- Pull weight directly up to your side, using your back and shoulder muscles with palms facing out.

- Return to the start position and repeat.

Workout A

A1. DB Split Squat

- Stand with arms at your side (or holding dumbbells with each hand) and one foot on a bench or step behind you. Squat down by flexing knee and hip of front leg until the knee of the rear leg is almost in contact with floor. Return to original standing position. Repeat. Continue with opposite leg.

A2. Spiderman Push-up

- Keep the abs braced and the body in a straight line from toes (knees) to shoulders. Place the hands on the floor slightly wider than shoulder width apart.

- Slowly lower yourself down until you are 2 inches off the ground. As you lower yourself, slowly bring your right knee up to your right elbow. Keep your foot off the ground as you do so.

- Push through your chest, shoulders, and triceps to return to the start position and return your leg to the start position.

- Alternate sides until you complete all repetitions. Keep your body in a straight line at all times and try not to rotate at the hips.

B1. Back Extension on Ball

- Lie across a stability ball with your feet extended and shoulder width apart and your hands behind your head. Your stomach will be positioned in the middle of the stability ball.

- Begin the movement by contracting your abdominals and lifting the upper body off the ball. Do not extend too far up into hyperextension.

- Return to the start position and repeat.

B2. Ball Rollout

- From a kneeling position, place your forearms on the ball with your palms facing each other.

- Take a deep breath and draw the navel toward your spine.

- Begin rolling forward, moving from the hip and shoulder joints equally. Maintain good spinal alignment as you roll forward. The movement should terminate the instant you feel you are going to lose spinal alignment.

Workout B

A1. DB Squat and Reach

- Begin in a wide stance with the toes slightly pointed out. Place the dumbbell in your right hand. Start in a squat position with the dumbbell on the ground.

- Raise your hand out above your head as you raise your body up.

- Bend your knees and lower the dumbbell back to the ground.

A2. Lateral Walk with Band

- Stand where you have room to move 10 to 15 feet laterally. Place a miniband around your feet and ankles so that it creates tension around your lower legs. Stand with good posture and knees bent slightly.

- Begin the movement by taking steps to the side while placing emphasis on your outside hip muscles. Try to make the steps progressively larger.

- Perform a separate set for each side.

B1. Bar Pull-ups

- Lie underneath a squat rack or Smith machine. Make sure to stack heavy weights on each side and/or check the stability of the bar before performing this exercise. It should not move from its position to ensure your safety.

- Grab bar with overhand grip just slightly beyond shoulder width. Place feet close together with heels against floor.

- Pull your chest straight up into the bar, lifting body with straight spine and tight abdominals, and then return to the starting position.

B2. Medicine Ball Rotations

- Sit on a 45-degree incline bench. Make sure your lower back is flat and your abs are contracted.

- Hold the ball directly in front of you at chest level, full arms' length away. Then crunch forward to a fully upright position.

- Rotate slightly to one side and then to the other.

Workout A

A1. Split Squat

- Start by resting your foot on top of a bench or small stool behind you. Place both hands on your hips and position your front foot so that your knee will not extend over your toes at the bottom of the move.

- Begin the movement by slowly lowering your body into a lunge position.

- Hold and then raise your body back to its original starting position by pushing through your heel.

- Repeat. Keep your stomach muscles contracted as you lower and then raise your body.

A2. Push-up to Hand Cross

- Start with your hands shoulder width apart on the ground and your upper body elevated. Your feet are slightly closer than shoulder width apart, and your lower body is elevated onto your toes. Keep your torso in a straight line.

- Take one hand and fold it across your chest while keeping your body in the same straight position. Keep your stomach muscles contracted throughout the movement.

- Return to the start position and then switch to the other hand.

B1. Lateral Walk with Band

- Stand where you have room to move 10 to 15 feet laterally. Place a miniband around your feet and ankles so that it creates tension around your lower legs. Stand with good posture and knees bent slightly.

- Begin the movement by taking steps to the side while placing emphasis on your outside hip muscles. Try to make the steps progressively larger.

- Perform a separate set for each side.

B2. Fit Band Cross-Body Rotation

Gym: Use weight pulley stack

- Position a cable machine at a low level. From a kneeling position, grab the handle with your outside hand and position the elbow next to your side.

- Pull the cable back as you rotate slightly away from the cable machine. If you do not have access to a cable station, use a fitness band.

Workout B

A1. Single-Leg Reach

Gym: DB Single-Leg Reach

- Stand straight with your body weight supported on your left foot. Tuck your right heel up behind you, with your lower leg roughly parallel to the ground and your right knee aligned with the left. Look straight ahead and don't arch or curve your back but maintain a neutral spine position.

- Flex your knees and hips to drop your butt toward the floor. Keep your chest lifted.

- Lower to the point where it becomes difficult to maintain your balance, pause, and push through the bottom of your foot to return to the start position. Make sure to do this in a controlled fashion.

A2. Cross-Body Plank

- Start with your hands shoulder width apart on the ground and your upper body elevated. Your feet are also about shoulder width apart, and your lower body is elevated onto your toes. Keep your torso straight and your body in a straight line without slumping or bending in the middle.

- Begin the movement by bringing in one knee toward the opposite shoulder. Keep your stomach muscles taut throughout the movement. You should feel a slight rotation in your hip and lower back as you move your knee across your body.

- Hold and then return your leg to the starting position.

B1. Fit Band Row

Gym: DB Row

- Sit with the legs extended in front. Begin by securing a band around your feet. Extend the arms in front of the body and hold the band with a neutral grip.

- Keep your elbows close to your side while using your back muscles to pull the band straight back.

B2. Side Plank

- Lie on your side on the floor with your elbow directly under your shoulder. Place one foot on top of the other in a stacked position.

- Push off your elbow and feet as you support your midsection in the air. Keep the body position in a straight line from shoulder to heel. Hold for 20 seconds on each side.

Golf Resources

Here are some excellent resources for golfers who want to learn more about how to become fit for golf.

Fitness for Golf

www.fitnessforgolf.com

A helpful website for extensive exercise programs, dynamic warm-up routines, and mental coaching strategies to play your best golf. Access to over 80 golf-specific fitness programs covering every level of golfer and background in exercise. Includes an interview section that contains interviews with other top golf fitness trainers who work with Annika Sörenstam, Phil Mickelson, Mike Weir, and other high-profile golfers. Maintained by *Going for the Green* coauthor Susan Hill.

Lean, Strong, and Long

www.leanstrongandlong.com

A customized program written by one of the foremost experts on fat loss that combines strength training and interval cardio training.

The program will help you burst through your past fat-loss plateau and build that coveted lean athletic body for golf.

Fitness-to-Play-Golf

www.fitness-to-play-golf.com

This is a great site if you are looking for golf fitness equipment to supplement your workouts. You can find golf fitness products as well as the newest technology advances in the field through handheld device downloadable programs.

101 Stretches for Golf

www.101stretchesforgolf.com

This book covers everything you need to know about how best to stretch for golf. Learn which stretches to do before you play and which ones you should do at home. Find out what it takes to restore the normal range of motion in your hips, back, hamstrings, and shoulders so that you are feeling refreshed and ready for the next round of golf.

Pod Golf Fitness

www.podgolffitness.com

Many golfers are looking for portable solutions to their golf swing problems. This comprehensive website offers exercise and stretch programs that can be instantly downloaded for even the most challenging swing issues.

Golf Fitness Challenge

www.golffitnesschallenge.com

Some golfers are looking for a new challenge or jump start for their game. This downloadable program offers physical challenges to every level of competitor, from recreational to seasoned pros.

Golf Training for Juniors

www.golftrainingforjuniors.com

For junior golfers, parents, or coaches in search of fitness training to help young golfers control more elements of their game and performance, this detailed manual by Susan Hill contains exercises, stretches, sports nutrition, and injury-prevention methods designed specifically for young golfers' growing bodies.

GolfersMD

www.golfersmd.com

GolfersMD, the official health and fitness content partner of the Golf Channel, is a new idea in specialized health information and the ultimate resource for golfers everywhere. It is the most comprehensive online golf health community—100 percent dedicated to injury prevention and treatment specifically for golfers.

Gary Gilchrist Golf Academy

www.ggga.com

The Gary Gilchrist Golf Academy helps junior golfers reach their full potential by offering them a proven training program that develops all aspects of their golf game, fitness, and mental strength.

Index

A

Action plan, creating, 31–34
Active rest and regeneration phase
      11, 163–166
  described, 11
  full program example, 15
  key elements of, 166
  mental game emphasis, 164–165
  physical game emphasis, 165–166
  technical game emphasis, 164
Alignment
  chipping direction and, 106
  defined/described, 60
  draws, 103
  drill, 60
  fades, 104
  on-tee evaluation and, 27–30
  overall instructional profile example, 30
  pitching direction and, 110
  putt chip drill, 116
  putting, 13
  sand play, 113
  as swing fundamental, 19, 27, 54–55, 56
All in one stretch, 135
Assessing round. *See* Post-round self-analysis
Assessment phase, 25–51. *See also* Golf fitness
      test; Physical assessments and evaluations
  described, 9–10
  full program example, 15

goal setting after, 50–51
key elements of, 51
mental evaluations, 31–36
technical evaluations, 26–31
understanding destination and, 26
understanding strengths/weaknesses and, 9,
    23, 25, 50–51

B

Back. *See also* Posture; Shoulders
  core structure and, 84–85. *See also* Core
  preventing injury to, 83
  stretching exercises, 91, 92, 93, 134, 135
Balance
  ground-based movements
    and, 81
  heels on board drill and, 74
  in life, 20
  losing, in downswing, 48
  in nutrition, 83
  plane drill for, 66
  principles of athletic development and,
    81–83
  stability and, 38
  standing dynamic balance test, 42
  static balance test, 45
  swinging club in, 56, 64–65, 83
  two-club balance drill, 68
  workout exercises for, 174, 180

Body fat
    calories burned and, 96, 97–99
    composition and nutrition, 96–99
    percentages, 48–49
Body motion, 61. *See also* Golf swing;
    Technical Phase references
Breaks, taking, 151
Bunker/sand play, 113–114

C

Caddy perspective, taking, 142
Calories burned, 96, 97–99
Challenges, accepting, 23
Champions, makings of, 26–27
Chipping, 106–109
Club awareness drills, 67–68
Clubs, 21
Committing to swing (shot), 122–125, 148
Competition phase, 141–160
    committing to shots, 148
    creating positive pressure, 153
    described, 11
    executing shots, 148–149
    focus of, 141–142
    full program example, 15
    how to score when it matters, 142–143
    key elements of, 160
    mistakes amateurs make, 143
    mistakes pros make, 143
    nutrition, 158–160
    perseverance in, 151–152
    physical game emphasis, 154–157
    planning shots, 146–147
    post-shot recovery, 149–151
    taking breaks, 151
    taking caddy perspective, 142
    technical game emphasis, 142–146
    tournament evaluation, 144–146
Conditions, assessing, 120, 127
Cook lift exercise, 89
Core
    anatomy of, 84–85
    endurance test, 41
    engagement test, 40
    importance of, 84–85
    physical fitness and, 83
    plank exercise, 86
    stability, postural control and, 83
    stomach pull exercise, 85–86
    training exercises, 84–86
Cross-body elevated plank, 87

D

Day-long microcycle, 12–13
Deep squat test, 39
Destination, understanding, 26
Diet. *See* Nutrition
Draw, hitting, 103
Dreaming, 5
Drills. *See* Technical phase drills
Dynamic stretches, 131

E

Equipment, about, 21
Executing shots, 148–149
Exercises. *See* Physical fitness
    training

F

Fade, hitting, 104–105
Fat. *See* Body fat
Finger down the shaft drill, 69

Fitness. *See* Physical assessments and
    evaluations; Physical fitness training
Flexibility. *See also* Warm-up routine; Warm-ups
    drills, 91–93
    hip stretch, 91
    importance of, 38
    kneeling midback stretch, 91
    lower-body stretch, 92
    lying back stretch, 93
    lying glute stretch, 93
    mental, 23
    shoulder and midback stretch, 92
Foot position. *See* Alignment; Technical phase
    drills
Forward and back lunge, 89
Four P's, 77–80
Fusser, Kai, 37, 50

G

Glute stretch, 93
Glycemic index, 158
Goals
    benefits of, 51
    dreaming and, 5
    focusing on, for winning, 23
    as key starting point, 9
    of periodization, 12
    post-round self-analysis, 170–171
    for practice, 126–128
    pre-round self-assessment, 169
    process-related vs. outcome-related, 126
    setting properly, 50–51
    of tournament play, 142
    understanding destination and, 26
    understanding strengths/weaknesses and,
      50–51

Going for the Green, program overview, 1–3
Golfer's seated rotation test, 41–42
Golf fitness test, 37–48. *See also* Physical
    assessments and evaluations
    core endurance test, 41
    core engagement test, 40
    deep squat test, 39
    flexibility and, 38
    golfer's seated rotation test, 41–42
    hip mobility/flexibility test, 46
    lower-body strength test, 47
    score breakdown, 48
    shoulder mobility and flexibility test, 43
    stability and, 38
    standing dynamic balance test, 42
    static balance test, 45
    strength and, 38
    swing fault identification, 48
    upper body strength test, 44
Golf fitness training. *See* Physical fitness
    training
Golf swing. *See also* Physical, and Technical
    Phase *references*
    basic ingredients of, 19
    commitment levels and results, 122–123
    committing to, 122–125
    fault identification, 48
    goal of, 19
    mental approach to. *See* Mental game
    new, committing to execution of, 122–124
    one-shot-at-a-time model and, 9, 11, 54,
      146, 149, 150, 151
    philosophy, embracing, 19
    post-shot recovery, 149–151
    post-shot routine, 152–153
    six steps of, 64–65

Golf swing (*cont.*)
    swing thoughts for, 142
    trusting, 124–125, 148
Golf swing revolutions (warm-up), 133
Grip
    drills, 57–58
    left-hand drills, 58
    on lob shots, 31
    moveaway drill, 67
    on-tee evaluation and, 27–30
    overall instructional profile example, 30
    pitching, 110
    plane drill, 66
    purpose of, 57
    putt chip drill, 116
    putting, 13, 117
    sand play, 113, 114
    split-handed drill, 70
    as swing fundamental, 19, 27,
        54–55, 56
    types of, 58
Grips (on clubs), 21

H

Hamstring-IT band standing
    stretch, 132
Heels on board drill, 74
Hip(s)
    glute lift for, 174
    mobility/flexibility test, 46
    restricted, 80
    rotation, 38, 48
    stretching drill, 91

I

Injury prevention, 83

J

Janzen, Lee, 36

K

Knee lift, high, 136
Kneeling midback stretch, 91

L

Lateral walks exercise, 88
Leadbetter, David, 36
Left-hand grip drills, 58
Lob shot drill, 115
Lofts, of clubs, 21
Lower-body strength test, 47
Lower-body stretch, 92
Lunges, 89

M

Mental game. *See also* Pre-shot routine
    about: overview of, 19–20
    active rest and regeneration phase, 164–165
    assessing conditions, 120, 127
    being present, 77–78
    comfort level of, 123–124
    committing to plan, 32
    committing to swing (shots), 122–125, 148
    common mistakes, 35–36, 143
    competition phase, 146–153
    creating action plan, 31–34
    creating positive pressure, 126, 153
    dealing with bad shots, 149–151
    evaluation form, 34
    evaluations, 31–36
    executing shots, 148–149
    focusing on others and, 35, 36
    four P's of, 77–80

full program example, 15

getting ego out of way, 36

how to play your own game, 35–36

insecurities, 35–36

observations to make, 35

one-shot-at-a-time model and, 9, 11, 54, 146, 149, 150, 151

patience and, 80

perception vs. reality, 31

planning shots, 146–147

positive attitude, 79–80

post-shot recovery, 149–151

post-shot routine, 152–153

pre-competition phase, 121–130

priming mind for success, 75–76

processing tasks at hand, 78–79

swing thoughts, 142

taking breaks, 151

taking charge of thoughts, 77

technical phase, 75–80

thought as basis of, 76–77

truth to accept about, 124

warm-up for, 125–126

Mickelson, Phil, 81, 151–152, 154

Midback standing stretch, 134

Motion, body, 61. *See also* Golf swing; Physical fitness training; Technical Phase *references*

Moveaway drill, 67

N

Nutrition

about: overview of, 20

competition phase, 158–160

glycemic index and, 158

key rules for performance, 158

performance-based snacks/minimeals, 159–160

physical fitness and, 83

pre-competition, 139

quick-release foods, 158, 159

slow-release foods, 158–159

O

Off-season. *See* Active rest and regeneration phase; Assessment phase

One-shot-at-a-time model, 9, 11, 54, 146, 149, 150, 151

On-tee evaluation, 27–30

P

Patience, 80

Periodization, 5–15. *See also* Periodization microcycles

beginning with end in mind, 9

defined/described, 2–3, 7

essence of, 9

factors that fluctuate, 9

full program example, 15

goal of, 12

length of program, 7

macrocycles, 7

phases of competitive golf and, 9–11. *See also specific phases*

regular tournament routine, 8

today's golfers and, 5–6

transitional preparation for, 11–13

Periodization microcycles

cycle lengths, 12

defined, 7

example of how used, 8

guidelines, 8

Periodization microcycles (*cont.*)
    one-day example, 12–13
    one-week example, 14
    sample putting practice, 13
Perseverance, 23, 151–152
Perspective, maintaining, 23
Phases of competitive golf, 9–11. *See also
    specific phases*
Physical assessments and evaluations, 36–51.
    See also Golf fitness test
    body fat percentages and, 48–49
    flexibility and, 38
    getting body "golf-ready," 48–50
    stability and, 38
    strength and, 38
    swing fault identification, 48
Physical fitness training
    active rest and regeneration phase, 165–166
    of Annika Sörenstam, 50
    Annika Sörenstam on, 37
    body fat, calories burned and, 96, 97–99
    competitive phase routine, 154–157
    complete pre-competition program, 136–138
    core training, 84–86
    cycle of, 166
    elements of, illustrated, 18. *See also specific
    elements*
    evolution of, 94
    exercise descriptions, 172–181
    flexibility drills, 91–93
    getting body "golf-ready," 48–50
    Golf Fitness Workout 1, 95, 172–175
    Golf Fitness Workout 2, 137–138, 176–178
    Golf Travel Workout, 156–157, 179–181
    importance of, 36–37, 80–81
    lessons from trainers of pros, 37

    for life, 165–166
    principles/guidelines, 81–83
    resources, 182–183
    rules of exercise progression, 84
    "Super 8" strength exercises, 87–90
    technical phase, 80–99
    Tiger Woods on, 37, 48, 49
    true power and, 80
    Vijay Singh on, 37
    warm-ups, 94
Physical game
    about: overview of, 19
    active rest and regeneration phase, 165–166
    competition phase, 154–157
    full program example, 15
    pre-competition phase, 130–139
Pitching, 110–112
Pivot drills, 62–63
Pivots, 61
Plane drill, 66
Plank exercise, 86. *See also* Cross-body elevated
    plank
Plank to a back row, 90
Planning shots, 146–147
Player development profile, 30–31
Positive attitude, 79–80
Positive pressure, 126, 153
Post-round self-analysis, 170–171
Post-shot recovery, 149–151
Post-shot routine, 152–153
Posture
    core stability and, 83, 84–86
    drill, 59
    focusing on muscles for, 48
    importance of, 59, 83
    inconsistent, as swing fault, 48

on-tee evaluation and, 27–30

overall instructional profile example, 30

poor, effects/common problems of, 83

putting, 13, 117

as "spine angle," 83

as swing fundamental, 19, 27, 54–55, 56

Practice, quality, 21

Practice routines

building schedule for, 121

changing clubs during, 127

changing targets frequently, 126, 127

creating action plan, 31–34

goals for, 126–128

one-day microcycle example, 14

one-week microcycle example, 14

practicing like playing/playing like
practicing, 120–121, 126–127

pre-shot routine during, 127

putting, 13, 127

real-life scenarios for, 120–121

sample practice weeks, 128–130

steps to incorporate into, 127

Pre-competition drills

chipping, 106–109

complete fitness program, 136–138

draw, 103

fade, 104–105

lob shot, 115

physical game emphasis, 130–139

pitching, 110–112

putt chip, 116

putting, 117–119

sand/bunker play, 113–114

Pre-competition (pre-comp) phase, 101–139.
See also Practice routines

committing to swing, 122–125

creating positive pressure, 126

described, 10

drills. See Pre-competition drills

full program example, 15

key elements of, 101, 139

mental game emphasis, 121–130

nutrition, 139

technical game emphasis, 102–119

warm-ups, 125–126, 131–136

Preparation, for periodization training,
11–13

Pre-round goal self-assessment, 169

Present, being in, 77–78

Pre-shot routine

assessing conditions, 120, 127

building, 120

in competition, 142, 147

considerations for, 120

example of executing, 147

full periodized program example and, 15

goals for, 126, 127

mental game, shot plan and, 146–147

one-shot-at-a-time model and, 9, 11, 54,
146, 149, 150, 151

patience and, 80

positive pressure and, 126, 153

practicing like playing/playing like practicing
and, 120–121, 126–127

practicing using, 127

using more frequently, 127

Principles of golf athletic development, 81–83

Processing tasks at hand, 78–79

Progression rules, for exercise, 84

P's, four, 77–80

Push-up to arm lift exercise, 87

Putt chip drill, 116

Putting
    drills, 117–119
    grip, 13, 117
    practice routines, 13, 127
    practicing with one ball, 127

R

Resources, 182–183
Rest, recovery, and regeneration, 20. *See also*
    Active rest and regeneration phase
Right foot back drill, 72
Rodriquez, Chi Chi, 17
Rotation
    common faults, 48
    fit band cross-body, exercise, 180
    flexibility and, 38
    flexibility drills, 90, 91, 92
    lunge with, stretch, 132
    medicine ball exercise, 178
    seated test, 41–42
    shoulder, stretch, 134
    warm-ups, 94

S

Sand/bunker play, 113–114
Scoring tips, 142–143
Seated rotation test, 41–42
Setup. *See also* Alignment; Grip; Posture
    chipping, 106
    with different clubs, 61
    importance of, 56
    key elements of, 61
    lob shot, 115
    on-tee evaluation and, 27–30
    pitching, 110
    putt chip drill, 116

    putting, 117
    sand play, 113, 114
    short game, 106, 108, 109, 110
Short game. *See also* Putting
    chipping, 106–109
    overall instructional profile example, 31
    pitching, 110–112
    sand/bunker play, 113–114
Shots
    committing to swing/shots, 122–125, 148
    executing, 148–149
    one-shot-at-a-time model, 9, 11, 54, 146,
        149, 150, 151
    planning, 146–147
    post-shot recovery, 149–151
    post-shot routine, 152–153
Shoulder and midback stretch, 92
Shoulders
    alignment of. *See* Alignment
    mobility and flexibility test, 43
    pivot drills, 62–63
    posture and. *See* Posture
    rotation exercise, 136
    stretching drills, 92, 134–136
    weakness in, 83
    workout exercise for, 175
Side stretch, advanced, 133
Singh, Vijay, 37, 154
Sörenstam, Annika
    dreaming and, 5
    mental game and, 20
    on physical fitness, 37
    strength/training of, 37, 50, 154, 165
    toughness of, 50
    trainers of, resource, 182
    weakness in driving distance, 37

Split-handed drill, 70

Squats, 39, 47, 84, 88, 94, 174, 175, 176, 177, 179

Stability, importance of, 38

Standing dynamic balance test, 42

Static balance test, 45

Statistics, analyzing, 27

Steps of golf swing, 64–65

Stomach pull exercise, 85–86

Strength

    fitness routine exercises, 172–181

    importance of, 38

    principle of developing, 82–83

    "Super 8" exercises, 87–90

Strengths and weaknesses, understanding, 9, 21, 23, 25, 50–51. *See also* Assessment phase

Stretching. *See* Flexibility; Warm-up routine; Warm-ups

Success

    characteristics of winners, 23, 151–152

    components of, 75

    makings of champions and, 26–27

    mental truth required for, 124

    perseverance and, 23, 151–152

    priming mind for, 75–76. *See also* Mental game

    in scoring, common elements for, 142–143

Support system, vii, 1, 20–21

Swing. *See* Golf swing; Technical phase; Technical phase drills

T

Technical evaluation, 26–31

    analyzing statistics, 27

    makings of champions and, 26–27

    on-tee evaluation, 27–30

    player development profile, 30–31

Technical game

    about: overview of, 19

    active rest and regeneration phase, 164

    competition phase, 142–146

    importance of, 19

    pre-competition phase, 102–119

    technical phase, 54–56

Technical phase, 53–99

    building foundation, 54

    described, 10

    drills. *See* Technical phase drills

    full program example, 15

    golf fitness emphasis, 80–99. *See also* Physical fitness training

    hallmarks of, 55

    importance of, 10, 54–55

    mental game emphasis, 75–80

    where not to place focus, 55–56

Technical phase drills

    alignment drill, 60–61

    body motion and, 61

    club awareness drills, 67–68

    finger down the shaft drill, 69

    focus of, 56

    grip drills, 57–58

    heels on board drill, 74

    left foot back drill, 73

    motion drills, 69–74

    moveaway drill, 67

    pivot drills, 62–63

    plane drill, 66

    posture drill, 59

    right foot back drill, 72

    setup, 61

    six steps of golf swing and, 64–65

    split-handed drill, 70

Technical phase drills (*cont.*)

    squatty 3-wood drill, 71

    two-club balance drill, 68

Thoughts. *See* Mental game

Tournament evaluation, 144–146

Travel workout routine, 156–157

Trusting your game, 124–125, 148

Two-club balance drill, 68

U

Upper body strength test, 44

W

Warm-up routine, 126, 131–136

    advanced side stretch, 133

    all in one stretch, 135

    golf swing revolutions, 133

    hamstring-IT band standing stretch, 132

    high knee lift, 136

    lunge with rotation, 132

    midback standing stretch, 134

    standing shoulder rotations, 134

    standing shoulder stretch, 135

Warm-ups

    dynamic stretches in, 131

    mental benefits of, 125–126

    physical benefits of, 125

    for physical fitness training, 94

    pre-competition, 125–126, 131–136

Website resources, 182–183

Week-long microcycle, 14

Wie, Michelle, 1, 30–31

Winners, characteristics of, 23, 151–152

Woods, Tiger

    Chi Chi Rodriquez on, 17

    on death of father and playing, 55

    dreaming and, 5

    of focusing on fundamentals, 55

    mental game and, 20

    on nutrition, 49

    periodization and, 2, 5

    on physical fitness, 37, 48, 49

    setting training trend, 17, 19

    support system, 21

    worthy of studying, 26

About the Authors

Gary Gilchrist

Overseeing the swing mechanics portion of the training program is Gary Gilchrist, owner and director of instruction of the Gary Gilchrist Golf Academy at Mission Inn Resort & Club in Howey-in-the-Hills, Florida. Formerly he was director of instruction for the IMG Academies/David Leadbetter Junior Golf Academy in Florida. In that capacity, he was responsible for recruiting and training some of the top young players in golf today including Michelle Wie, Sean O'Hair, Paula Creamer, Casey Wittenberg, Virada Nirapathpongporn, Chan Song, Aree Song, Naree Song, Candy Hannemann, David Gossett, Ty Tryon, and Christo Greyling. His work with David Leadbetter allowed him to oversee the training of top tour players such as Nick Price, David Frost, Nick Faldo, Mark O'Meara, and Andy Bean.

He also served as director of instruction at the International Junior Golf Academy in Hilton Head Island, South Carolina. His current clients include Suzann Pettersen, Julietta Granada, Shanshan Feng, Nicole Perrot, and European PGA Tour star Peter Hedblom, who says of Gary: "He's pretty special. He's more than a technical coach; he knows so much about everything, especially about how you should prepare. I think that's his strength. He wants you to have confidence in your game, not just in your teacher."

Susan Hill

As president of www.fitnessforgolf.com, the leading web-based company specializing in optimal training programs for elite-level golf competitors, Susan Hill is on the cutting edge of this movement.

Susan is a certified Golf Biomechanic Sports Performance Nutritionist, Fitness Trainer, and Youth Conditioning Specialist. She was recognized as one of the top three trainers in the country as selected by the International Sports Science Association in 2003 from a pool of over 85,000 candidates. Her work has been featured in *Golf Illustrated*, *Travel Golf*, *Junior Golf Scoreboard*, *SELF* magazine, *Atlanta Golfer*, *Pacific Northwest Golfer*, *Resort Living*, GolfersMd.com, and on ESPN. She has directed the golf fitness program at the International Junior Golf Academy, where she was responsible for overseeing the training of more than 150 competitive junior golfers. She has served as the golf fitness consultant to the Colombian Golf Federation in South America. She currently works with college golf teams, competitive amateurs, and tour professionals.

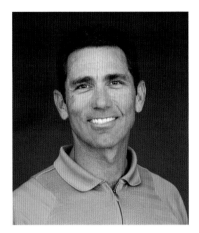

Jeff Troesch

Having served as Director of Mental Training for the David Leadbetter Golf Academies, Jeff Troesch's experiences have allowed him to develop a methodology that produces golf champions around the world, using the mental component of training. In addition to having worked with top professional and amateur golfers including Jill McGill, Brittany Lang, Jason Buha, David Gossett, Thongchai Jaidee, Michael Allen, Candie Kung, Angela Park, Jane Park, Anthony Kim, Jennifer Osborne, Irene Cho, and Mina Harigae, he also serves as a consultant to golf programs at the University of California–Los Angeles, the University of California–Berkeley, and California Polytechnic State University.

"I see my role as a knowledge broker, who takes all the elements and then helps the player put together a plan of action," he says. As the mental side of the game is often what holds good golfers back from further achievement, Jeff's role is critical. Jeff has worked with players on the PGA Tour, LPGA Tour, Nationwide Tour, Futures Tour, Asian Tour, European Tour, Tight Lies Tour, Hooters Tour, Gateway Tour, and AG Spanos Tour.

Jeff Troesch's work is also not limited to golf. He has been a consultant to several teams and organizations, including Major League Baseball's Seattle Mariners and Detroit Tigers, the National Basketball Association, the U.S. Soccer Federation and its Women's National Team, and many other professional, collegiate, and amateur sport programs. He is also a regular speaker for many golf-related and other sport association events, including the American Junior Golf Association. He resides in Southern California.

Picture Credits

All images by Alan Huestis unless otherwise noted below:

ii © Shutterstock/Joe Mercier

vi © Shutterstock/Palych1378

2–3 © Shutterstock/Dallas Events Inc

4 ©Shutterstock/FloridaStock

22 ©Shutterstock/Sebastien Burel

28 Courtesy of Wikimedia Commons/Golf Course
Scotland.jpg/Author: Turan Rajabli

94 Courtesy of Wikimedia Commons/Heavy
Dumbbells 200 pound.jpg/Author: LocalFitness Pty Ltd.

96 Courtesy of Wikimedia Commons/Military cyclists in
pace line. jpg/Author Airman Nathan Doza

100 ©Shutterstock/Junker

140 ©Shutterstock/Chad McDermott

154 ©Shutterstock

159 ©Shutterstock/Maksim Shmeljov

160 ©Shutterstock/Ovidiu Iordachi

161 ©Shutterstock/Benis Arapovic

162 ©Shutterstock/rfx

167 ©Shutterstock/Galyna Andrushko